Successful Women In Busi

Successful Women In Business - Leadership Edition

Successful Women In Business – Leadership Edition

Successful Women in Business – Leadership Edition

Edited by Jacqueline Rose

Published by Lovely Silks Publishing 2022

Research by: Delphine Beaumont, James Morgan, Sarah Chapman and Gregory Blackman

Originally Published by Lovely Silks Publishing 2016

Research by: Sarah Chapman, James Morgan, Katerina Smith, Gregory Blackman and Olivia Cartwright.

Successful Women In Business Leadership Edition

Successful Women In Business – Leadership Edition

Published by Lovely Silks Publishing 2022

All rights reserved. No part of this work may be reproduced or transmitted in any form or by any means, electronic or mechanical, including photocopying, recording, or by any information storage or retrieval system, without the prior written permission of the copyright owner and the publisher.

This book is presented solely for educational and entertainment purposes. The author and publisher are not offering it as legal, accounting, or other professional services advice.

While best efforts have been used in preparing this book, the author and publisher make no representations or warranties of any kind and assume no liabilities of any kind with respect to the accuracy or completeness of the contents and specifically disclaim any implied warranties of merchantability or fitness of use for a particular purpose.

Neither the author nor the publisher shall be held liable or responsible to any person or entity with respect to any loss or incidental or consequential damages caused, or alleged to have been caused, directly or indirectly, by the information or programs contained herein.

No warranty may be created or extended by sales representatives or written sales materials. Every company is different and the advice and strategies contained herein may not be suitable for your situation. You should always seek the services of a competent professional.

Successful Women In Business – Leadership Edition

Sharing Some Thoughts From Some Of The Contributors:

My voice is often soft but the words I say are strong. After all, women having opinions is a wonderful thing that can only benefit us all.

Junko Kemi - From The Boardroom To The Catwalk

Life is good, not because I'm jet setting around the world but because when I come home, I do so to a loving family. A home of giggles, happy children and a husband that appreciates the life we have together, a real man who loves my children like his own, and in laws that mean the world to me.

Lorena Öberg - From Self-Doubt To Self-Accomplishment

Life is indeed unpredictable and forever changing, but it also offers endless opportunities for those who are ready to embrace them. So make sure you are ready.

Suzi Chen - Curating Your Success

Stay focused on what you believe in. It sounds obvious, maybe a little cheesy, but I have often repeated this mantra to myself over the years, especially when things get tricky.

Emma Coleman - From Nurse to Holistic Skin Specialist

We have built up a very recognisable brand, and by some referred to as an institution. This has been achieved through dedication, hard work and a passion for educating others and ourselves, not being afraid to fail and being innovative.

Linda Stewart – More Than Just A Salon

Whilst it is crucial to work towards a healthy profit margin if a business is to make a change in the world for good, that company must have a healthy perspective on what will benefit its customer, its suppliers and the community at large.

Judith Treanor - Profit Or Purpose And Personal Fulfilment?

Starting a business with not much money is an achievable and rewarding path to success. Anyone that believes in themselves, and believes in their goals, like I did, can find their way into their own exciting venture. Find your own genius and create value for other people and you will find yourself skyrocketing to success.

Catherine Craig -Starting A Business With No Money

Learn To Celebrate Yourself - guess what? You are not perfect. And you know what? You don't have to be. Learn to accept yourself and love yourself. Don't beat yourself up for all your failures and weaknesses instead; celebrate your strengths and successes.

Christine Khor - Create the Life You Want

Don't forget to Embrace-Life, Love and Each Other.

Rosie Shalhoub – Embracing Rosie

Successful Women In Business – Leadership Edition

The Thought Leaders Who Contributed To This Book:

Chris Roberts MBE, Carly Hooper, Marie Friend, Gen Edwards,

Junko Kemi, Honey Lansdowne, Lorena Öberg, Debi Wallbank,

Tamika Martin, Rosie Shalhoub, Alexa Doman, Christine Khor,

Renee Catt, Suzi Chen, Emma Coleman, Linda Stewart,

Judith Treanor, Catherine Craig, Rebecca Carroll-Bell

Successful Women In Business – Leadership Edition

Table Of Contents

Welcome To Successful Women In Business	17
How To Turn Adversity Into Success	19
Changing Career For My Son & His Future	30
Harmonic Egg Healing	40
The Dream - And My Business	50
From The Boardroom To The Catwalk	57
How Self Discovery Creates Business Success	68
Self-Doubt To Self -Accomplishment - Lorena Öberg Story	83
Menopausitivity	94
Made For Success	104
Embracing Rosie	112
Find Your Way To Professional Fulfilment With Confidence	130

Create The Life You Want	144
Defining Success	159
Curating Your Success	167
From Nurse To Holistic Skin Specialist	177
Building More Than Just A Salon	188
Success: Profit Or Purpose And Personal Fulfilment?	199
Starting A Business With No Money	213
Finding Out What Being Successful Really Means	223

Welcome To Successful Women In Business - Leadership Edition

Women entrepreneurs are rarely satisfied with the status quo: Instead they strive to build the world in the way it should be rather than abiding by a system that's potentially archaic or outdated. During the course of researching this book we have come to realise that breaking down barriers for women in the workplace is key to success for companies and for countries.

That's the message we hope you will pick up from this book. When more and more women are seen at the top of organisations and running high growth technology businesses, the more this will be regarded as the standard and a perfectly normal, and logical, path to choose.

Starting a company, or managing a company through a period of transition and growth, can be a riveting roller coaster of emotions with tremendous highs and at times, difficult lows. But despite the challenges, many women have risen to become leaders and influential figures in their respective areas.

Successful Women In Business Leadership Edition recognizes and celebrates the outstanding contribution made by individual women to their businesses and, in many cases, their local communities. The business leaders profiled in this book are of various ages, social backgrounds and industries. However, the one common thread which unites them is that they dared to believe. And, in believing, they made the seemingly impossible a reality.

Their individual stories tell of the challenges we all face: uncertainty, fear, discouragement, hope, commitment and yes, that indefinable, illogical and yet all-consuming belief that we will succeed against all odds. These are real-life individual stories of success that I hope will also encourage you to believe and to make that difference.

Jacqueline

Jacqueline Rose

Editor of The Energy Healing Magazine &
Equilibrando – Your Health & WellBeing Balanced Magazine

How To Turn Adversity Into Success

I'm used to writing stories about other people, but here is a rags-to-riches story about me and my journey from a dysfunctional and dead-end start in the world to a life of achievement and happiness. It's about how I made things happen to better my lot in life and achieve relative success. I hope it might serve as an inspiration to anyone who is struggling in their business or personal life to show that you really can turn a negative into a positive.

I didn't have the best start in life as my mother was dying and didn't even know she was pregnant. So my entry into the world was not planned and was a total surprise! Not only had my mother been given just three months to live, she was also unmarried and out of work! In 1948, when I was born, being an unmarried mother carried a huge stigma in society and was distinctly frowned upon. These were a lot of hurdles for her to overcome and for me to deal with whilst growing up. With these handicaps, how was it possible for me to take my first step on the ladder of success and get to where I am now?

My life as a child consisted of doing without a lot of the things that other children take for granted and, as I had to spend a lot of my free time helping and looking after my bed-ridden mother, I didn't have any friends and hardly ever spent time in the company of my peers.

When I left school at 16 and was thinking about going to college and what I should study, I told my mother that I wanted to be a journalist. In those days, there were no career advisers – boys went to work in factories and girls became shorthand-typists. My mother's reply to me was "You need to get a proper job and be a secretary!" In her mind, being a secretary was a step up from being a shorthand-typist and far better than being a journalist! So, over the years, I had various shorthand-typing, secretarial and personal assistant jobs, but was always the thwarted journalist deep down inside! It was always in the back of my mind that I wanted to write.

I knew then that I had to carve out a different life for myself to the one my mother envisaged – I had to move away from my birthplace and start a new way of life. My philosophy has always been that if you want something badly enough, you can get it. My motto or strap line is: "I can make things happen" – and I can! I really can! I always tell people that they too can make things happen if they are determined to succeed and turn any opportunity that arises to their own advantage. I think my determination to succeed is probably as a result of being an only child and always being used to getting what I wanted! This has continued into my adult personal and business life and second best is just not good enough for me. Why accept second best? Why not strive for perfection and make your life, home, job, relationships the best that they can be. I am a perfectionist and believe this is definitely a plus point to nurture. Going for gold is so much more fulfilling than winning bronze or silver!

Around 40 years later in 2000, my own children having grown up, I got my first job writing a weekly column in the local newspaper – the Wilts and Gloucestershire Standard (or WAGS for short). Since then, for the past 27 years, I have written regularly for WAGS and ad hoc for many other newspapers and magazines – hence WAGS, rags and mags!

I actually call myself a freelance journalist and facilitator as, not only do I write press releases for people, businesses, organisations and events, but I also help with facilitating fundraising for community groups and, 15 years ago, I founded and was the facilitator for a Business Club that now supports hundreds of businesses across Gloucestershire, Oxfordshire and Wiltshire.

Soon after starting my journalism journey, I got involved in community work and also became a Town Councillor and District Councillor as well as being elected Mayor of my town. With these links to other organisations, one thing led to another and I started making a name for myself as someone who had her finger on the pulse and knew at first-hand what was happening in my area and was, therefore, also able to write about it. I started writing, editing and publishing a Newsletter for the Town Council; then started writing and editing a Newsletter for the Business Club I founded as well as notching up more local magazines and newsletters on my belt.

I don't claim to be an expert on business or promoting businesses but, over the years, I have learned a lot and now find myself in a position to utilise my experience to help others. When I first decided to start a Business Club, someone said to me: "This has been tried before and didn't work." Well that was like a red rag to a bull and it gave me the impetus to start up a Club and make it successful. So, I advertised that I was holding a meeting for business owners who may be interested in networking together for mutual support, and was elated and encouraged when over 80 business owners turned up to the first meeting. Running the Business Club enabled me to find out what makes businesses tick. What they want from customers, suppliers, advertising and marketing. And what works best for them to get the best promotion for them and their businesses.

I am still a Town Councillor; I am also a Gloucestershire Ambassador for Business (GLAM for short!) and a Switch on to Swindon Ambassador. I still write every week in my local newspaper, but the original weekly column has now grown to a whole page; I also have a monthly Business page in a local magazine; and, a year ago during the pandemic, with so much marketing work coming my way, I took the decision to create a 'proper' PR and marketing business under my own name: Chris Roberts MBE PR.

Yes! Chris Roberts MBE – as I was thrilled to have been awarded an MBE by HM The Queen in her 2009 Birthday Honours. It was one of the most glorious and memorable days of my life being presented to Her Majesty, chatting to her and receiving my medal in front of my husband, daughter and son. I was bursting with happiness, yet was sad that my mother had not lived to see the day and discover how successful I had become.

Before starting my Chris Roberts MBE PR business, I had mostly written articles, press releases and articles for free! It was for me a way of doing what I loved doing and also giving back to my town community *and* business community.

However, when I first started my business, a successful PR guru friend of mine told me that I needed to start charging for what I did and not undervalue myself. Previously, most of my PR work was done philanthropically – my contribution to the community. But my friend explained to me that if you give something away for nothing, it appears to have no value. Yet, if you put a price on your service, then it becomes worth something of value. My Chris Roberts MBE PR business has proved even more successful than I ever imagined, especially as I had not envisaged anyone actually wanting to pay me for what I did! I now have a number of clients that I write for on a regular basis; new clients wanting to engage with me each week and I continue to produce my regular WAGS, rags and mags pages.

In addition, I have very recently started to contribute bi-monthly to a successful woman's online magazine and have also embarked on another new business project. This will involve interviewing people about their life and then capture their life story on camera for them to pass on to their loved ones as a legacy of their life after their death. I boast that 'I poke my nose into other people's business and then make up stories about them'. And I do! I love hearing about people's lives, businesses, events and then promoting them with their unique, interesting stories. Very often, stories are more powerful than paid adverts to promote what you do and who you are, because stories evoke emotion, are more engaging, they build rapport and relationships.

If I was to create an advert about say a photographer and wrote that this particular photographer is experienced in child photography, portraits, animals or weddings, then you probably wouldn't be overly interested as you have heard it all before, and many other photographers can claim the same thing. If, however, I wrote a story to say that this photographer had won an award for a beautiful photograph of a child picking daisies in a meadow, then your interest would increase. It paints a lovely picture in your mind. If the story then went on to say that this child was the son or daughter of a well-known celebrity, then you might be even more interested and maybe even consider using the photographer yourself. This is how the right story can make a powerful impact. Sadly, or maybe fortunately, not everyone deals with celebrities, but every business has an interesting story to tell. It's just a question of finding the interesting hook!

Previous clients have told me that the press releases I write encourage more customers to their business and that they love seeing their names in print in the media and social media. My new clients have certainly discovered this for themselves and I have a page of glowing testimonials to prove this! Since starting my business in October 2020, I have been very busy. I never like to say 'no' to anyone, so will always try to fit a new or existing client into my schedule. I work very hard and quite long hours, but I enjoy what I do and get a real buzz out of making someone happy with a story that has been published for them. My job is a labour of love and something that I am pleased to have made happen after my initial desire to become a journalist 57 years ago!

So, what do I love about my business? Well it would probably be quicker to ask what I don't like, as there is very little. Long before the pandemic, lockdown and the requisite working from home, I was working from home through choice. I love being in my own home environment and not having to get in the car and drive anywhere on motorways or in the rush hour. I can have a tea/coffee/lunch break whenever I want; I can also be there when the post delivers a package that has to be signed for; I can hang the washing out on the line and then hurriedly bring it in if it starts to rain. There are so many positives about working from home.

I think the main perk of my job is meeting so many lovely people either actually (pre-Covid) or virtually (post-Covid) and listening to what they have to say. The majority of people are only too happy to talk about themselves, their businesses or their interesting – often unique – stories. Armed with a few questions to ask them, I generally find that people are usually more than willing to give me as much information as possible about themselves or their business in order for me to create a magnificent promotional article for them.

After interviewing my victims – sorry I mean clients! – I really enjoy getting their feedback on the draft I have written for them, even if this needs changing somewhat sometimes. Their input is very relevant and necessary. I pride myself on being 'an ethical journalist' i.e. I don't go for sensationalism or dishing the dirt. I like feel-good stories that make you smile and feel warm inside. I enjoy seeing or hearing about their reaction when they read their story or promotion in print for the first time. It is their moment of fame and is exciting for them and me. Finally, probably the best bit for me is getting a positive and glowing testimonial which makes me smile, warms my heart and which I can use to promote my own business.

One such testimonial I received recently said: "You are a super star, Chris. Thank you for believing in me and being a driving force in getting my business started by writing your wonderful words." Another testimonial I loved, but haven't yet taken advantage of was from a coffee shop owner, who said: "I just wanted to say thank you for the article you wrote in this month's magazine. It was a lovely read and great for my little business. The afternoon teas have been a massive hit and you must book yourself in to try one!"

I love every single minute of every single day being a writer, journalist and promoter of businesses, people and events. My business – Chris Roberts MBE PR – gives me so much fulfilment and pleasure especially as I love making things happen for people as well as poking my nose into other people's business and making up stories about them!

One particularly successful article I wrote was an interview I had with Sarah Pinborough, the author of the book *Behind Her Eyes*, a supernatural psychological thriller that was made into the No. 1 Netflix six-part series. I had worked with Sarah in the past, so decided to contact her about her book and Netflix success and asked to interview her. The interview then got picked up by *What's on Netflix* magazine, who then posted it on their website and in their Newsletter. Quite a coup!

I have been asked quite often what I believe is my greatest achievement. That's easy! It was receiving my MBE (for services to the community of Fairford) in 2009 from HM The Queen at Windsor Castle. It was incredible

Successful Women In Business – Leadership Edition

receiving my MBE in the historic Waterloo Chamber and seeing at first-hand many of the beautiful rooms in Windsor Castle with their ornate furnishings, embroidered carpets, gold-detailed carvings decorating the walls and gold trim on the ceilings, stunning chandeliers and original fine art everywhere.

I did manage to remain not too over-awed when Her Majesty spoke to me, asked me questions and laughed at some of my responses. She made me feel very comfortable which enabled me to forget I was speaking to and shaking hands with the most famous woman in the world! When I heard that I was going to receive an MBE, I really wanted it to be the Queen who presented the honour, as I had met Prince Charles, Prince Phillip and Princess Anne on previous occasions. And I really wanted to receive it at Windsor Castle, because I had previously been to a Garden Party at Buckingham Palace and wanted a different Royal venue! So, was it cosmic ordering, mind over matter or the power of positive thinking that gave me what I wanted or was it just luck? Probably a bit of everything.

It could also have been the fact that I had put my desire to be awarded with an MBE on my bucket list of the top ten things to do before I die. It is definitely extra beneficial to have a goal at the forefront of your mind or on paper and try to achieve it – something to strive for, accomplish and then have the satisfaction of crossing it off your list. The thrill of knowing you have achieved something will then spur you on to the next thing on your bucket list.

Looking back on the successes and achievements in my life, I think I can put these down in part to my dysfunctional childhood – being brought up as the only child of a terminally-ill, financially-strapped, single parent! A psychiatrist would probably diagnose that I suffer from 'only child syndrome'. Children with this syndrome can be spoiled, selfish, self-absorbed, bossy, but also have advantages such as achievement, intelligence and creativity.

Throughout my life, I have nearly always managed to be successful at job interviews and with sitting and passing exams. With interviews, I seem to have an in-built insight into the employer's perspective and seem to know the right thing to say. I am able to read people and understand what they want and then interact with them. Exams were relatively easy for me at school, not because I was inordinately intelligent, but because I had a knack of being able to think outside the box to give an innovative answer that the examiner would like. Always try to think on your feet and don't give the answer that people expect you to give – something original always grasps people's attention and leaves a lasting impression.

I believe that I have managed to be resourceful and determined and not to accept the hand that fate originally dealt me. And the 'only child syndrome' really does seem to have worked for me and has made me try much harder in life than I might otherwise have done.

It is this philosophy that has helped me become relatively successful in life. My dysfunctional childhood and early life illustrates that anyone can overcome hard times; anyone can defy the odds and use adversity as a reason to find the strength and determination to build a better life. I escaped a life of being brought up by an ailing and sometimes bedridden single parent on benefits in a Council house in the rough end of town to living in a lovely home in a beautiful part of the country with a well-respected business, comfortable life-style and enjoying family life with my husband of over 40 years and the two children that I always wanted.

I believe that I have managed to beat the odds and have made good, positive things happen for me. Anyone can do this too if they want it badly enough.

By Chris Roberts MBE PR

About The Author

Me At Windsor Castle Collecting My MBE With My Daughter, Sarah; Husband, Dave And Son, Adam In November 2009

I am a freelance journalist, writer and promoter of businesses, people and events in Gloucestershire, Oxfordshire and Wiltshire. I enjoy poking my nose into other people's business and then making up stories about them. Having lived in the Cotswolds for over 40 years, I've been writing about businesses, people and events for many of those years through newspapers, magazines, social media and newsletters.

I've previously written and edited a bi-monthly Newsletter for Fairford Town Council; written, edited and published a monthly Newsletter for a Business Club; written monthly stories for a local magazine; and had articles in other magazines and newsletters. I currently write a weekly page in the Wilts & Glos Standard; a monthly business page in Faringdon's The Advertiser magazine and a bi-monthly business page for Empowered Magazine. My latest venture is with My Life Film, writing someone's life story ready for filming and produced as a legacy of that person's life after their death.

In 2000, I was co-opted as a Town Councillor and became the Mayor of that town from 2005-2007. I was then elected as a Cotswold District Councillor, where I served from 2007-2011.

In 2006, I founded a Business Club to support businesses throughout Gloucestershire, Oxfordshire and Wiltshire and introduced their annual Awards event.

During lockdown in 2020, I helped launch The Cotswold Challenge to create an educational activity for 15-19 year old students who had missed their GCSEs and A-Levels. I'm an experienced fundraiser and have been involved in helping community projects and charities raise hundreds of thousands of pounds. I am a Gloucestershire Ambassador for Business supporting the local economy and a Switch on to Swindon Ambassador. I received my MBE in 2009 for my work in the community and my strap line is: 'I can make things happen'.

Successful Women In Business – Leadership Edition

To Find Out More Visit

Chris Roberts MBE PR

E: chrisrobertsmbe@gmail.com

W: www.chrisrobertsmbe.co.uk

FB: www.facebook.com/ChrisRobertsMBE.PR

Twitter: @ChrisARoberts

Instagram: chrisrobertsmbe

LinkedIn: Chris Roberts MBE

Changing Career For My Son & His Future

Successful Women in Business, what a fabulous name for a book, what an inspirational read this will be. However, how do we define success? Is it by the amount of income, is it by company turnover, number of employees, number of products sold, number of awards won or is it something else?
I like to think it is something else and I think I actually have that something else………..I am still working on the income and the big turnover part though!
I went to university to study a joint honours in Psychology & Criminology and within a few weeks knew this would be the career for me. I was interested in the criminal mind and in particular the reasons a larger proportion of men commit crime than women. Fast forward a few years and I was employed by a university on a project for the Home Office whilst working on a PhD. I was motivated, passionate and loved the work I did. Having been told I'd struggle to have children but with a husband wanting nothing more than to be a dad we began what we thought would be a long journey to parenthood. It wasn't! Within a few weeks I felt unwell and discovered I was pregnant.
Everything was text book. An easy pregnancy, I carried on working but stopped prison visits once the baby bump was obvious. I agreed maternity leave with the university but would carry on my PhD studies as much as was possible. Our baby boy made a surprise appearance four weeks early, a lovely 6lb 13oz his early arrival was put down to him being a good size while I am quite petite. Totally smitten first time parents we began the baby journey confident, calm and full of hope. Like many first time parents we had an antenatal support group and with our baby boy arriving earlier than all the others we expected our milestones to be ticked off before anyone else. This however was not to be. As the months went on the gap in development

between Callum and the other babies got wider and wider. He took longer to focus his eyes, to smile, to roll and did not sit up until he was nine months. Health visitors blamed his four week early arrival and assured me he would catch up. We had also noticed he failed to use his left arm and hand at all and actually kept the left hand in a clenched fist. If we forced him to use it, he struggled, he appeared unable to reach with it or engage the hand to grasp toys. It was then I was told he was lazy and "obviously right-handed". Totally unhappy with such an explanation I asked to be referred to a paediatrician. A four month wait when you're eleven months old is a very long time so we paid privately to have an appointment in the next few days. Within two weeks our "obviously right-handed and lazy" baby had been diagnosed with Hemiplegia. He had a brain scan and was found to have had a stroke at 27-32 weeks gestation resulting in extensive damage to both sides of his brain, particularly the right. The result was Hemiplegia, a condition caused by brain injury that results in a weakness on one side of the body, a stiffness or spasticity and a lack of control. Hemiplegia is a relatively rare condition, affecting up to one child in 1,000. About 80% of cases are congenital (before, during or immediately after birth), and 20% are acquired. Hemiplegia affects each child differently. We were told that Callum's brain damage was so extensive he would probably not walk or talk. I was mortified at this attitude, there was no way I was going to have my child immediately written off so I politely informed the consultant that she'd never met me before and that we'd see in a few years whether Callum would walk or talk. Needless to say he does both with a lot of vigour.

This diagnosis changed the course of our family life and in particular my life. I decided with little hesitation that there was no way I would be leaving all the extras Callum would need to a third party. I needed to do his physio, his speech and language therapy, his occupational therapy work, I needed to give him the best possible chance of being the best he could possibly be. I therefore resigned my position at the university but continued with my PhD which I finished around the time he was diagnosed – if memory serves me

correctly I had my viva the morning we were taking him to see a neurologist for his final diagnosis……..talk about stressful!
I was already working part time for another university marking MSc essays which they sent me online so I continued to do this when Callum slept. Our days were full of singing, stories, sensory play, physiotherapy and anything that I thought would aid his development. At two and half years old he started at an Early Years setting in a Special School which he loved. He is still at that school and is a strapping 5' 11" fifteen year old, still loving school. His baby brother Patrick arrived in 2009 and despite our concerns and also arriving early he is neuro typical and a distinctive qualities of a boy!
Fast forward to 2012 and I decided to get involved in beekeeping. I read a magazine article about a couple keeping bees in London, this sparked a real interest for me. I bought a book, joined my local Beekeeping Association and completed their beginner course. Whilst learning about keeping bees I also read instances of beeswax being used in cosmetics and health care. I wondered what else I could do with my new found love of beekeeping and turn it into something more, something that would fit round my family. I read how honey had been used on wounds during the first Word War due to its healing properties. Already loving all things natural and having an appreciation for alternative therapies and suffering with really dry hands in the winter I wondered if I could produce a beeswax and honey based product that could heal and protect my sore hands. After weeks of research and trial and error I made a honey rich balm that worked wonders on my hands. Patrick's eczema happened to flare up so I tried it there too and within three days of using the balm it had disappeared. So I looked into what else I could make and investigated the market for beeswax and honey based skincare. I made lip balms and a honey soap, distributed them across my friends and was delighted with the positive feedback I received.
The positive response, the support and encouragement of my husband and my own sense of ambition resulted in me launching Beeutiful in November 2013. The brand is based on water-less body balms and butters. I chose this route as I wanted to avoid using preservatives, as my research had revealed

many people were intolerant to the preservatives in their beauty products. I wanted my range to be suitable for all skin types but particularly sensitive and dry skin. Balms and butters are oil based and therefore extremely hydrating. The addition of beeswax locks moisture into the skin as well as providing an almost waterproof protective layer, again perfect for those with sensitive and dry skin.

I launched with ten products including three lip balms, body butter, honey soap and my hand saviour product B-balm. I hired a room at a local hotel, borrowed a microphone, invited everyone I knew and got them to bring everyone they knew and had a launch party. I had a visit from the local press with a promise to be in numerous local rags and there began my journey to get Beeutiful into the hands of people with a preference for natural skincare. With Beeutiful launched, I worked around my two boys. With Callum at school and Patrick my youngest at pre-school I focused on growing my brand locally. I became stocked in two local shops, attended local markets, local school events and built up a reputation in my area, so much so I am now known as the Bee Lady.

Beeutiful is now eight years old and I've managed to grow the brand whilst being the mummy to my two boys that I always wanted to be. I have purposely grown Beeutiful slowly and organically. I have not thrown lots of money at it in terms of a huge marketing campaign and branding as I needed to stay within boundaries that meant I could still attend my children's needs. I didn't want to oversell myself or over-stretch my time as to me the children and in particular Callum's additional needs had to come first. I am very lucky and I will be the first to admit it, that I have the full support of my husband. Both emotionally and financially he has supported this journey and he appreciates everything I do. I joke that if I were to drop dead tomorrow he would have no idea who had to be where, when or in what clothes. However he carries the financial burden of providing the roof over our heads and the food on the table. My earnings from Beeutiful have become our fun money, our holiday fund and finances the presents to ourselves.

I will also be the first to admit that it is a juggle, a real intense juggle and I do start my day early and end it far later than most people. However, between the hours of 3pm and 8pm very little Beeutiful work is done. That is Mummy time. I pick Callum up from school, he requires snacks, assistance with personal care and entertaining. I oversee Patrick's homework, nowadays also calling him to see what time he will be home, warning him it's now getting dark, asking," where are you?". Then ferrying him to afterschool activities. I cook dinner, and like my thoughts on skincare I have strong thoughts on meals too. I've been a vegetarian since I was 13 and strongly believe that what you put in your mouth is super important. I therefore cook from scratch every night. My idea of fast food is veggie sausages and mash. I receive a weekly fruit/vegetable box so whatever is in that I turn into a meal. This therefore means we are also eating seasonally, better for the environment on so many levels and better for us. Of course it can be a challenge, coming up with meals, (who has time to study recipe books, I just create with what I have), using what is in the fridge, tick the box for three (if you include husband) hungry boys and produce something that doesn't take three hours of cooking. However I also take pride in what I do and if a job is worth doing then its worth doing properly, I am a real believer in this and spout it out loud almost daily!

So the juggle is real, the early morning starts, trying to cram some admin work in whilst the rest of the house is asleep, clock watching during the day to ensure I'm ready on time to pick Callum up from school. Doing the family/house stuff 3-8pm and then returning to the work once Callum is in bed. Luckily Callum loves his sleep and mostly once he is in bed, he is in bed. I therefore am free to engage in making product in my workshop which is in a converted part of our attached garage. Working this way gives me a big length of time to focus and concentrate on product making so I immerse myself in the process totally.

Callum is now 15 and although not much more independent than when he was a toddler he has progressed really well and I feel all my hard work in the early days post diagnosis has really paid off. We were told he would not walk or talk, I am delighted he does both! Putting in all that extra care, giving up my career to focus on him is a decision I would take again tomorrow. Looking to the future my husband and I are putting measures in place to expand Beeutiful in different ways. We have bought a 14 acre field with plans to cover it in bee hives, run beekeeper experience days and of course sell honey. Almost daily I am asked to supply honey but with my current 15 hives all the honey is required for the Beeutiful products. In addition with thoughts turning to creating a small holding we currently have eight rescue chickens that happily roam around a 25 metre square area, from which I supply three neighbours with eggs. Just like the honey I have other potential customers as well as two local retailers who would be delighted to sell our organic free range eggs. We will therefore invest in 250 rescue chickens over the coming few years. We have also planted crops with plans for more next year

Where Callum will be in a few years I have no idea, whether he will hold down a job I am not sure. If he does I foresee he will need close supervision, maybe still need assistance with personal care and therefore will require a full time carer. Our vision is that our small holding will create a job opportunity for him. Whether it be feeding the chickens, collecting eggs or counting jars of honey into boxes how amazing would it be to know we have provided an opportunity for him to have a level of independence. The ultimate dream is to live on site and have a shepherds hut or log cabin for Callum with us right next door, again a level of independence but with us there as security and assistance.

What started as something to provide me with a career, an income and follow my quest for achievement I hope will turn into a provision for Callum to lead as "normal" a life as possible. To have a job, to have his own home but also still be assisted as and when required I see as a dream scenario. As a family we are to embark on a whole lifestyle change, a change that will provide for both our children but importantly provide an income for our child who faces more challenges than most. Importantly his younger brother is very aware of the challenges Callum faces and understands that we are putting things in place to assist him. He of course is a huge part of that and wouldn't it be great if one day he took over the small holding we dream of building, but if he doesn't then he doesn't and hopefully we can have it managed by others whilst the boys are able to still own it, providing that essential income for Callum. At the moment this is all ideas, wishes and hopes, who knows how it will turn out. What I do know though is that I have started something that I will not give up on, that has the potential to be huge for my family and provide security for my child who has an uncertain future ahead of him. This is not something we envisaged or planned fifteen years ago but I work very much on the pretext that you're dealt your cards in life so take them, run with them and make the best of them for you and those around you. I think that is exactly what I am doing with our current plan and I am very proud of that.

I am super proud of what I have achieved, super proud of the forthcoming plans and have every confidence we will achieve what we currently envisage. What it takes though is hard work. Hard work, determination, grit and a refusal to accept a negative outcome. I disagree wholeheartedly when someone is written off or when someone says something can't be achieved. You can achieve anything you want to achieve, be anything you want to be but you have got to work at it.

My advice to any parent starting a business whilst caring for a family is to put the hours in, it will be a juggle, it will feel harder than being a simple employee but just imagine that sense of pride when your children say mummy or daddy runs X business or when you are able to employ your child within your business, offer them some security. I'd say to anyone debating whether to give it a go, I'd say do it, just do it but be prepared to put the work in and you will be rewarded.

This brings me full circle back to my introductory paragraph on success. What is it, how do you measure it? Is it based on turnover, income, profit, number of employees or is it something else? I think it is far more personal. Success to one is not success to the next person.

Successful Women In Business – Leadership Edition

I feel I am a successful business woman as I have created and run a business whilst caring full time for my children, one of whom has additional needs. I have attended all his medical appointments, school activities and engaged in hours of additional care and work with him, all of which has enabled him to be where he is today.

That is something I am proud of and so yes I would say I am a successful business woman as that success is defined by the achievements and happiness of those around me not simply by the number my business may or may not turn over.

By Carly Hooper

About The Author

Carly is 44 a mum of two boys, married to Andrew living in Fleet, Hampshire. She runs her business Beeutiful from home, is training manager for Fleet Beekeeping Association & Chair of the PTA at her son's special school. She is also an avid gym goer & marathon runner. She lives her life with the belief that you can be anything you want to be, that nothing is impossible & you can achieve anything you put your mind to. Having left her career as a forensic psychologist she now keeps bees, produces natural skincare & has big plans for a smallholding that will employ her disabled son & perhaps provide a place of interest for other SEN children & adults to visit or even be employed.

To Find Out More Visit:

www.beeutiful.co.uk

www.facebook.com/beeutifulskincare

www.instagram.com/beeutifulskincare

Harmonic Egg Healing

After a very traumatic end to a 25 year relationship which spanned from 17yrs of age, a marriage and two children I found myself in what some may call a dark night of the soul. Feeling utterly bereft and at a loss of how to find happiness (as my beloved Dad passed away 5 months after my marriage break up) I began to realign with the person I once was as a young girl and started to practice meditation…. this was 10 years ago almost. My two children were 8 and 13 years at the time of the breakdown and to say it had a devastating effect on us all is an understatement.

My meditation practice led me down lots of other esoteric subjects that I was also intrigued about as a young girl and my interest and energy in this area continued to grow and develop. I became much more interested in Neuroscience, Epigenetics and anything to do with the mind body connection. I had an overall thirst for subjects of a spiritual nature I was just engrossed in humans as a species, what made us tick, why we behave the way we do and what other factors / information is available in the field that we just can't see with the naked eye. For as long as I can remember I have always felt that there was much more to this life than what we had been led to believe. I vividly remember experiencing consciousness as a child but was never able to articulate it.

Six years later life was starting to feel a little more settled when life decided to throw me another curve ball when the family business that provided my income took a downturn and it became apparent that my income was about to completely disappear. I had to put my house on the market and move in with my Mum for a period of 6 months whilst once again I found my feet and worked out which way to go from here.

By this time my kids were 15 and 19 and once again I found myself saying, "we'll get through this don't worry". The difference this time was that whilst what was happening was utterly devastating and frightening I had an innate knowing that this was all happening for a specific reason and that better things were to come. It felt like another dark night the soul and I were left wondering why? I was being pushed to the limit when once again I felt like I had lost everything.

During the time at my Mums I got myself attuned to Reiki and my intrigue and further studying deepened yet again. It was at this time my son had started to suffer with his mental health, diagnosed with anxiety and depression and it was probably one of the most challenging times of my life. Any parent knows that when your child suffers there's no stone you won't turn over to look for a solution. Being more of a holistic person and with all my knowledge and interest in Neuroscience I knew he was suffering from emotional trauma from our marriage breakdown. He was at that tricky neurological age 7/8 when it happened, the brainwaves are the softest and I knew that that trauma would hardwire as well as store in the tissues and manifest itself somewhere down the line. This it most certainly did.

Eventually I found a house to live in, moved in and continued to manage the challenges faced when your loved one is suffering from a mental health issue, which seemed to be lasting forever. Jointly my son and I decided not to go down the pharmaceutical route and I spent every waking hour looking for alternatives.

I came across The Harmonic Egg in the USA. A sound and light vibrational frequency chamber that created an environment to heal the mind and body. When I started to research The Harmonic Egg it blew me away. I was convinced this would help my son and not only him but it could help so many other people not just with mental health concerns but so many other things. This resonated with me on every level.

By this time a global pandemic had swept the world and during the lockdown period I began to study Anatomy and Physiology so I had a better understanding of the body and its functions which dovetailed nicely with all the holistic and energy methods I had acquired. The thought of having a Harmonic Egg would not leave me and whilst I kept pushing the thoughts away (I was absolutely in no financial position to be purchasing an Egg), but the thoughts kept resurfacing.

I Knew I had to ask for guidance on this one as my rational mind was saying absolutely not but my heart was saying yes. After months of replaying it in my head and a few zoom calls with the Inventor Gail Lynn (as well as receiving all the signs I asked for) I found myself applying for a massive corporate loan to finance the purchase of a Harmonic Egg. To my amazement I was granted the loan and the process of communicating with the USA during a pandemic began. Getting this Egg across the ocean in a pandemic to the UK wasn't going to be easy. I couldn't even get to the USA to "try before you buy" with all the travel restrictions in place at this time. But something in my gut told me to carry on.

So without even trying it out first I was fully into the process of setting up Harmonic Egg Healing still unsure of the exact date of its arrival. The pandemic was making everything unsure and unsteady, could we even get it onto the Ocean and over to the UK with what was going on?

Divine timing couldn't have been more perfect when my Harmonic Egg arrived at Liverpool docks (not without additional dramas of course). The docks of Liverpool were backlogged tremendously and they physically couldn't get to the crates containing my Egg. Meanwhile I had the manufactures of the Harmonic Egg from the USA sitting waiting ready to build and install it. As events turned out my youngest brother offered to drive to Liverpool with his open back truck and after borrowing a forklift we managed to get the crates back to Chester after two journeys and tons of praying.

The Harmonic Egg was finally installed at the end of April and I opened the doors to Egg Healing 1st May just as we came out of lockdown. My first two clients came from London. I'm now 7 months down the line and it's still very much early days but the word of The Harmonic Egg has reached far and wide with clients coming from all over the country. What I'm witnessing day after day never ceases to amaze me with the profound effects the Egg is having on people. It's not for the faint hearted setting up a business that no-one has ever heard of before or understands what it can do for them but the energy I receive from the people who come through my door literally lights me up every day as I watch their transformation and hold space for their profound experiences.

The Egg seems to have its own consciousness and treats each and every person uniquely and individually and will always deliver what is needed to the recipient. it might not be what you want but it will definitely be what you need as the Egg delivers the opposite frequency to your imbalance always. At the time of writing this piece I am seven months down the road of first opening the doors to Harmonic Egg Healing. What I'm witnessing never ceases to amaze me, each person has a unique experience in the Egg and every day delights me how people describe what they feel, their experience whilst in the Egg, and how it goes on to affect their life moving forward. I always explain at the outset that it's very much a healing journey, which begins with an autonomic nervous system reset. Then we start to get to the point of what we are trying to address, and how we plan to get to the root of problems, whether that be something to do with your belief system or a very real condition such as a fibromyalgia.

I'd Like To Share Some Of The Experiences My Clients Have Had:

Shelly (name changed to protect anonymity) who had suffered a traumatic sexual event in her earlier life, followed by a toxic abusive relationship, as a result of this she had been suffering with severe anxiety and had recently had a breakdown. She had tried counselling for a period of time but when the counsellor suggested she try something else as she was detached from her body with her mind the sessions were not having any effect.

Her Mum had contacted me as Shelly's anxiety was so bad that she felt unable to contact me herself. At her first appointment with me she was unable to look me in the eyes when I spoke to her. She answered me by looking at her mum when replying to my questions. I could clearly see she was in a high state of fight or flight and her nervous system was completely sympathetic and unbalanced, being intuitive I could clearly pick up on her energy, there was much trauma.

I explained the protocol for the session and informed her how the session would go. She would be in the Harmonic Egg for 50 minutes, 40 minutes surrounded by sound and light and 10 minutes of silence whilst the body integrated the experience. The music inside the Egg is specifically composed for the Egg and is not music heard before, this often releases emotions as different sounds activate different parts of the body. I informed Shelly this may/not happen and to release any emotions that come up, it's the body's way of releasing trauma, like a detox it needs to come out as suppressed emotions and trauma often stores itself in the tissues and manifest as disease somewhere down the line. After the 50 minutes session was up I opened the door to the Egg to find Shelly with the broadest smile right across her face.

She came out and sat back down on the sofa in my office and both Shelly and her Mum could not stop laughing. "Why are you laughing" her Mum asked. "Mum you need to get in there, it's amazing" Shelly beamed. She literally could not stop grinning, she couldn't explain why or how she felt so good and so different. I can't explain how it feels as the facilitator of The Harmonic Egg and how it lights me up to see such a different change in energy to clients before and after a session in the Egg. Shelly's Mum messaged me the next day to say that she could not stop smiling all night after her session.

Fast forward to Shelly who now uses the Egg regularly as part of her healing journey and after 5 Egg sessions she has been able to come off her medication, comes to Egg herself without her Mum and continues to flourish and grow. The change I see in the woman who attends now from the person who first came through the door never ceases to amaze me. Like everything in life it requires maintenance and a commitment, but the benefits in this particular case are outstanding as Shelley is truly able to move forwards in her life as we work on releasing the trauma of the past.

I particularly enjoy listening to the variety of experiences people have in the Egg, from those who say they felt a definite connection with a loved one who had past and felt it hugely comforting. Or those who feel absolute clarity and focus on certain things in their life and those who feel the absolute joy and relief of a deep relaxation on a completely different level that never before have they felt.

The visuals of colours and scenes people describe to me has me sitting open mouthed and very appreciative of their shared experiences. Whilst no two are the same some common threads do get stated such as "I felt pressure in my crown chakra ". "I felt like a heavy pressure in my heart was lifted". "The colours and shapes I saw blew me away my creative mind went wild". "I felt a deep sense of peace and calm like I've never felt before". "I saw a scene played out with people I don't know and I don't know what it meant"

"I felt so heavy like I couldn't even lift my arms" "I was so relaxed I couldn't move". There's also a large portion of people who can't even articulate what they have just experienced and sit there for a little while dazed and confused as to what actually happened. After all, for most people it's an experience in which the body has never been in before so it's no surprise that people can't fully understand or explain what has happened. A common thread is that people lose all track of time in there and can never judge how long they have actually been in the Egg. I always say that time doesn't exist when you're in the Egg as you're catapulted to a different place altogether.

I recently had a professional snooker player come to have a session. This was a gift that was bought from him by his sister, so he had no idea what to expect or what it was about really. I briefly told him about the science behind sound as a way to affect the body at a cellular level and how colour also affects the mind and body and that he would be surrounded in 360 degrees of both sound and light, along with the fact that the design of the Egg was based on Tesla Mathematics and sacred geometry. In short there was a lot to this modality. He shared with me that he was open and willing to try. He was looking for something to quiet the mind as he had a very important match the following week, so anything that could ease the mind chatter and put him at ease for this upcoming event, which required absolute focus and concentration. He loved his session, couldn't really articulate how he felt or the experience he had just had but knew he felt good and different.

The following morning I had his coach on the phone who also wanted to block some sessions in the Egg and to know what this was all about. On his arrival he went on to tell me that my client won his match and the coach then proceeded to tell me in his next session the following week that in a friendly match he himself had got his highest break on the table in six years. He smirked as he repeated the pro snooker players comment, "That's the Harmonic Egg for you".

The change in my client's energy when they come out of the Egg for me is palpable, along with a completely different appearance, they glow, their faces soften and their hearts more open, eyes are brighter. People are always asking me how The Egg works. I explain how sound healing affects the body and the brain. It's believed that resonance may be the most important principle of sound healing. Everything has a frequency at which it naturally resonates. This is known as Prime Resonance Frequency (PRF). Our bones, cells, and organs all have their own PRF.

For example the PRF of a typical cell is 1000 hertz, whilst the heart is around 100 hertz. The resonance principle relates to the cellular absorption of the healing sounds and / or their harmonics. In sound healing, resonance principles are employed to re-harmonize cells that have become unbalanced as a result of toxic substances, emotional traumas, or pathogens, etc. In 2015 Dr Dominic Surel a professor at Energy Medicine University California, also a member of the Society for Scientific Exploration and co- founder of the World Institute for Scientific Exploration shares evidence from a slew of scientific studies which show that:

- Listening to music releases endorphins, which increase the body's tolerance to pain and reduce stress.
- 30 minutes of classical music produces the same effect as 10mg of valium (Baltimore Coronary Care Unit Study)
- A study published in the Journal of Paediatrics in April 2013 looked at what happened when Mothers sang lullabies to premature babies.

Monitors showed that the music reduced the stress levels of the babies, their heartbeats slowed down, they became noticeably calmer and oxygen saturation increased.

This is just a very small example of the many scientific studies that have been conducted about sound and how it affects the body as well as how colour therapy works and how coloured lights slip beneath our conscious awareness, reaching beyond the cerebral cortex. It penetrates our emotional and memory centres while triggering significant psychophysiological responses. Ultimately, freeing us from our past traumas.

Within the chamber of the Harmonic Egg light, frequency, vibration and sound create a blended energy to stimulate one's autonomic nervous system to reorganise and promote homeostasis. This natural meditative relaxation state is risk free and has no side effects compared to pharmaceutical agents. This therapeutic form of energy is now being called "Frequency Medicine" by new Science. Scientific contributions from neuroscience, molecular biology and physics are now actively supporting energy or frequency medicine as a legitimate alternative.

As the first person to bring this modality to the UK I can only say the last 7 months have been a multitude of emotions, uplifting, challenging, frustrating, joyous, exhilarating and everything in between. What is clear to me is the energy of my clients this has not only kept me going but it has lifted me up as I share and hold space for their experiences and their stories that they share with me. I'm beyond grateful. The power of human potential and shared love for each other is a point of reference I continue to bring myself back to.

By Marie Friend

About The Author

Marie Friend is the owner of Harmonic Egg Healing in Chester UK. She is the first person to bring the Harmonic Egg from the USA to the UK, the wheels of motion were set during the lockdown of the 2020 pandemic. She is a single Mum to an 18yr old son, 23 year old daughter, a dog and two cats and lives in Cheshire.

Marie has worked in the Media, photography and hospitality Industry to name a few. Trained in Reiki, Anatomy & Physiology, Broadcast Journalism and a guided meditation facilitator Marie has an avid interest in all things energy, esoteric and cosmic disclosure.

To Find Out More Visit:

https://harmonicegghealing.co.uk/

The Dream – And My Business

Lots of people – me included – have big dreams. And so many of us struggle to follow the dream, because it's so scary, and so overwhelming, and it feels like, 'I'll never be able to do this.' And so, we just get on with it, we get on with living our lives, and still we dream, that one day, it'll all happen. Well, I'm here to tell you, that if you're ready to keep putting the work in, and keep believing in The Power of You, your dreams can come true. Mine started to come true at 62, and, for a long time before that, I had thought they never really would.

I was adopted. Adopted at birth, into the most wonderful, loving, supportive family – and yet despite all that, I seldom felt 'good enough.' For much of my adult life, I also never believed I could be successful. In my 50s, I met a financial advisor, a coach and a healer. The financial advisor, being delightfully atypical, (in my experience to date) told me about a coach and an energy healer, thus proving to me in hindsight that when the pupil is ready, the teacher appears.

I started working with the coach – she was primarily a business coach, who also ran family constellation sessions. Family constellation sessions – if perhaps you've not heard of them – are powerful healing workshops where volunteers act as family members, working with the client to represent a particular family dynamic. They are highly intuitive sessions, guided by a facilitator, and may result in wonderful, deep, healing experiences. Parallel with this, I started working with the intuitive energy healer, who, the first time she worked with me, completely astonished me by asking, "Who abandoned you?"

Her intuitive picking-up on my adoptive story made me feel that there was potentially something profound in what she could do for me. Now was the time for me to start working through my story, through my past, and rewriting it to become a person who *was* enough.

Working in parallel with the action steps my coach was pushing me to do to expand my Training and Development consultancy, I was doing self-development work such as affirmations, journaling, Gratitude work and reflecting. She encouraged me to start moving out of my comfort zone and showed me how small, incremental actions could result in big changes over time. She taught me to take actions that were aligned to my overall dream and vision of where I wanted my business to be. Looking back, the biggest takeaway for me, has to be that it's wonderful to have a dream of what I want, but unless I'm prepared to put the work in, it will always be just that – a dream. I'm so grateful to my coach, for encouraging me to go where I didn't necessarily want to go, and for holding a safe space for me to grow in.

Alongside my coaching and self-development work, I was also getting regular intuitive energy healing. I started noticing, over time, that I was feeling happier and happier. Not that I had noticed being 'unhappy' previously, but I noticed now that I was inclined to often feel optimistic, and that things felt like they were going my way. And because I loved the energy healing experience and results so much, I started wondering if I could do it too, and I began reading books on the subject, and experimenting. And so, I started learning how to feel into it. I worked on myself, as my own guinea pig, and then on friends and family members, as I became ever-more fascinated by the results intuitive energy healing offered.

Because I wanted to 'do it properly', I enrolled for the training of my chosen modalities, and started working through the certification processes. This was time-consuming, because I had to document several healing sessions and submit the records for examination, in addition to completing an online knowledge assessment. Through it all, though, I was feeling pleased and excited about what I was learning.

I achieved my first qualification, and started work on the next. I was working with people in the evenings and on weekends, and the idea started creeping in – maybe this could be a full-time business opportunity? I began dreaming, then, that my passion might turn into a successful business in the future. I've now been in my business full-time since January 2020. Given my current age, given my complete change in direction from adult learning and development to intuitive energy healing, I honestly feel that it's never too late. My business kept on going regardless of the Pandemic, and it allows me to do the things I want to do, in the times when I feel like doing them. I imagine I'll be doing this for many years to come, because I love what I do and I can't see myself stopping. *Cheers To Financial Advisors*

Things I Would Tell Someone Who Wanted A Successful Business:

1. *Find Your Passion.*
2. *Practise Building A Positive Mind-set:*
   Building a positive mind-set is key to success because it allows us to expect the best possible outcomes instead of the worst. Ways to build a positive mind-set are to catch, switch and ditch negative self-talk statements that pop into our mental and verbal speech, to keep a gratitude journal and remember how much we actually do have, to be grateful for. This leads us to focus on the good things rather than the things that make us feel unhappy. Apart from anything else, studies show that optimistic, positive people are often healthier and have better stress-coping mechanisms.
3. *Work With A Coach As Soon As You Can Afford To:*
   My coach really helped me separate the wood from the trees in terms of helping me get clarity around my vision and what I wanted to do. This is a skill that I've carried forwards, even though I no longer work with her. Working with a coach gives you access to a different point of view, she had different insights and suggestions and was able to give me some fresh perspectives. Having a coach gave me a really supportive, positive and safe space to grow and make mistakes, and she challenged me too, suggesting and encouraging me to do things I never would have dreamt I could do. You could work with a coach as little as once a month, if affordability is an issue.
4. *Surround Yourself With Positive People:*
   Form a support group, or a Mastermind group, of like-minded people who also want to be successful in their businesses. Meet regularly and cheer each other on. Sometimes, family and friends may be a bit dismissive and have an attitude of 'You'll never make it', and if that's the case with you, find support and

acknowledgement elsewhere. Initially, it's a possibility that you'll be working from home (depending on what your business offers) – it can be helpful to work from a shared office space once or twice a week, just to get out of the house and to be working with other small business owners.

5. ***Join Networking Groups:***
Networking groups are wonderful to help you get your business exposed to other people, or to other businesses. After the Pandemic, many networking groups have kept some of their meetings online, which means you could potentially meet people from all over the country – or indeed, the world. Apart from that, it's fun to meet people in other small businesses and to learn from them. Some networking groups offer coaching, and business skills training, and they're a great place to find people you can outsource to – things like your website design, or your social media posts. I outsourced both of these jobs as soon as I could because neither one of them bring me any joy and I prefer to work on my core skills, leaving other tasks to people who enjoy them.

6. ***Make Sure You Have Some Kind Of Income To Support You When Just Starting Out:***
I would recommend doing this, because at the start, if you don't have enough clients to bring you the kind of money you want, it will be very stressful and it may cause anxiety to watch bills mount up and wonder how you'll pay them. I did a transition job – I moved into a retail store and worked part time before launching my business full time. This way I built up clients and while I did so, still brought in money.

7. ***Don't Give Up Too Soon:***
Typically, it will take time to build your dream business. It's very easy to feel like it's not working, no-one is noticing, you don't have enough clients. If you're passionate about your idea and love what you're doing, then I'd recommend be realistic in your expectations. Studies show it can take the first three years just to find your feet, establish yourself and find your direction. Running a business is hard work, and can be lonely, so hang in there and believe things will improve.

8. ***Celebrate All Your Successes:***
    Sometimes we're so driven to achieve something that when we do, we almost overlook it in readiness to achieve the next thing. Stop. Take time to celebrate your wins and acknowledge what a great job you did.

When I was deciding whether or not to create a new venture at age 62, I realised that time would pass regardless – whether or not I created a business. I could choose to get older and try to achieve what I wanted, or I could choose to not give it a shot. After all – you never know 'til you try, do you?

By Gen Edwards

About The Author

Gen is a former Zimbabwean living in West Yorkshire with her husband and dog. She enjoys the beauty of the English countryside and of being able to tramp around taking in scenic walks and beautiful surroundings.

She has been practising Energy Healing since 2015, primarily using The Emotion Code and The Body Code, both of which she is qualified in. She helps people all around the world with physical, emotional and mental illness and disease – facilitating their shifting from pain to peace, from chaos to calm – whatever that looks like to them. She loves the challenge of figuring out tough issues that no doctor seems to be able to budge.

If You Want To Find Out More:

You'll find lots of Healing Case Studies on Gen's:

Website: https://www.genedwards.com/

Gen is active on many social media platforms

Face Book: https://www.facebook.com/GenEdwardsBodyCode

From The Boardroom To The Catwalk

Humble Beginnings

Ever since I was a little girl, I've always wanted to be my own boss, and the responsibility of having my own company excited me. I wanted to lead and inspire others to create new and innovative products that would make people happy and put a smile on their faces; I wanted to create 'new value'. As a youngster, I didn't have a definitive plan of what my business would look like but looking back I guess it was obvious that I would enter the retail sector. After all, I was following in the footsteps of my beloved grandmother, who had the most influence on me becoming a businesswoman. Growing up, I spent a lot of time with my grandmother in her kimono shop in Osaka. She was kind, never complained, always helped others and achieved anything and everything she put her mind to - in short I thought she was so cool and wanted to be just like her.

As a retailer, customers appreciated her honesty and her flexible style of working for example, convenient opening hours and custom made clothes. With a child's enthusiasm, I would pretend that I was a customer walking around the shop, looking at how she could improve the business, from what suited customers to the colours and design of the fabrics adorning every shelf. Although she always listened to me she did not always take my advice.

Teenage Struggles And Finding My Voice

The teenage years are a struggle for a lot of young people and sadly I was no exception. When I was around 14 or 15 years old, I failed to gain a place into my first choice high school (ages 12-18) and disliked my substitute choice. Whilst I can look back now and see that everything worked out for the best, at the time, this was devastating news for me, especially in the academically competitive environment of Japan. I lost a lot of confidence in myself, felt I wasn't good enough, didn't believe in my abilities and consequently really withdrew into myself.

I, like many teenage girls, placed a lot of pressure on myself, to succeed at everything I did and to fit in with my peers. The turning point for me came when I was 18 and one of my closest friends passed away from cancer. During our friendship, he provided me with much needed support, gave me confidence, believed in my abilities and told me that I was unique. At his funeral, I suddenly realised that life is far too short and that it passes by very quickly. I knew that I needed to be more confident, and concluded that for me to achieve my goals, the most important thing was to grab every opportunity and work as hard as I possibly could. Armed with this new attitude, my life changed for the better.

Shortly after, I began my degree at Waseda University studying Western History. While I was at university, I began hosting charity fundraisers and awareness events relating to the prevalence of HIV in Japan. This was a very topical and sensitive issue at the time due to a series of high-profile medical accident cases in which a group of young people were infected with HIV. Organising these events helped me to find my own voice, as I felt empowered by playing a part, even if it was a small part, in ensuring that students were better informed and in turn, better protected.

Entering The World Of Work

Upon graduation, my first job was with as a sales representative with Benesse, an education publishing company, in Osaka. Whilst I had a burning desire to establish my own company, I used this role to develop my basic skills and learn as much as I could in the areas of sales and marketing. By suggesting ideas for schools to tailor products to their students based on feedback from educational professionals, I was able to grow and be very creative in this role.

This experience of acting on customer feedback would prove invaluable in setting up my own companies in the future. My confidence at this time grew considerably and helped me gain real life skills. I went from being a total City girl to traveling around remote parts of Japan by myself and learning how to progress in a very male-dominated environment.

Aged 25, I decided that I wanted a new challenge, and I made the decision to leave Benesse for a role at the professional services firm, PwC. The nature of PwC meant that I learnt new skills in areas as diverse as accountancy, law and consulting, and my marketing skills came in handy as well! A short turnaround on projects became the norm, meaning I had to become adept at learning, accessing and analysing quickly on the job. The time I was at PwC was certainly an opportunity in which I was able to grow and solidify my experience and skills.

I've always believed that it is important to continually challenge yourself and your capabilities, so I decided to branch out further at Boston Consulting Group (BCG). As one of the biggest consulting firms in the world, BCG was the ideal place for me to learn more about the processes of business and to work alongside individuals from all walks of life, cultures and disciplines.
Initially, I found the role a challenge as I was working primarily in the medical and IT industries – a real departure from the education sector. However, I was ready for the challenge and excited at the opportunities to grow both professionally and personally. BCG's mantra is how to get maximum results in the shortest amount of time, which is crucial when you are working under tight deadlines and to high expectations. This was a useful learning point when I established my first business as I suddenly realised I would have to multi-task like I had never multi-tasked before.

Becoming My Own Boss

My boss at BCG was a very smart man, and he had observed and met many professionals in his time. He explained to me that my strengths were in marketing. Coming from someone with so much experience and high standards, these words were very powerful for me and helped me to formulate my future plan. Another former colleague encouraged me to take steps to find new clients, stating that once I had found three, I should resign from BCG. I took her advice and began to identify potential clients through my networks and social media. Soon, I had three clients, in IT, insurance and energy. After a lifetime of imagining and preparing, I started my own marketing consultancy business in 2008, five years after I joined BCG.

Starting Again

I loved owning my own business – yes, it was incredibly hard work with lots of travelling and even more late nights but, seeing my business thrive and grow was the most rewarding feeling in the world. The company was called 'Maojian Works,' which is Chinese for my family name 'Kemi'. The reason I chose a Chinese name was because I had identified areas of growth for my business being outside of Japan, with China being a future key region.
On Friday 11th March 2011, my life completely changed. That day, I was in Nagoya, in the middle of a presentation to a client. The day was the day of the Great East Japan Earthquake and tsunami. The Tohoku earthquake once again made me realise how short life is, and after running my marketing consulting business for five years, I began reflecting on a piece of advice my grandmother gave me, "life is not about how much you make; it's about what you leave behind."

With this in mind, I thought of ways in which I could improve the lives of other women while also tapping into my interests and passions. An idea took hold based around the fact that I would often struggle to find clothes that worked with my busy professional life. You may not think it would be difficult to find practical and comfortable yet also elegant clothing in a city as large as Tokyo, I would spend my precious free time walking around malls and department stores for suitable work attire, only to return home empty handed. I wondered why the larger clothes companies were not catering to the professional female demographic and it was this moment that kay me, a fashion brand for businesswomen by a businesswoman was born.

Buoyed by excitement and a newfound energy, I began in earnest to answer two key questions - how do I produce a dress? And how do I ensure that women buy kay me dresses? My friends, who have been incredibly supportive, recommended a tailor and his advice was to collaborate with an excellent pattern cutter. Through the power of social media, I was introduced to a wonderful pattern cutter who not only creates beautiful garment templates but also has connected me to a wide range of industry professionals, suppliers and trading companies. She has and continues to be imperative to the kay me journey and I am proud to say she is now a partner in kay me.

During this time, I liaised with my network to hold focus groups, where I interviewed future kay me customers and showed them samples of potential products. This included an event at my former employer, Benesse where I presented the first collection to my fellow professional women and received some very useful and honest feedback. Feedback on areas including price and design was extremely valuable and helped me to shape and refine the collection, ensuring that the samples met all their requirements.

In my opinion, focus groups are extremely important and a valuable way of gaining insights from your core audience. However, if you are asking for advice it is important that you listen to any feedback given whether it is positive or not. It is never easy to listen to criticism; it does usually help the business in the long run.

By May 2011, just eight weeks after I had initially contacted the tailor, I had 40 samples and was fortunate enough to hold a launch party at a luxury hotel in Tokyo. Using my marketing skills, I was able to attract a large crowd with all of my dresses selling out on that first day. As you can imagine, I was delighted – a real highlight of the kay me journey so far.

In July 2011, I opened a showroom and invited customers to book appointments to view the collection. The showroom was located in an area close to Tokyo's financial district, making it easy for professional women to come and view the clothes at a convenient time for them. The showroom was so successful that after two months, I created an ecommerce platform and delivery service.

In 2012, kay me took a significant step forward when I opened my first bricks and mortar retail store in Ginza, Tokyo. Ginza is one of the most exclusive areas in Tokyo, equivalent to London's Mayfair or Fifth Avenue in New York and as a result, it was risky to launch in such a high profile and expensive area. However, it was vital that kay me launched in an area, which reflected our target audience, and I was so proud when the shop opened in September. Since then we have gone from strength to strength in Japan, and now have five bricks and mortar outlets. In addition to our flagship store in Ginza, we now have one in downtown Osaka, another at Haneda international airport and concessions in two Tokyo department stores.

Going International

2016 has been the year that we have really started to focus on expanding our horizons internationally. London was first on our agenda due to its talent pool, multiculturalism and the access it gives to other global cities including New York and Singapore (both of which are also on our hit list).

The first thing I have learned about how to launch in a new territory is to get the input and advice of people who are native to the country you are planning to launch in, because they will be able to provide insights into the local culture that you might miss. The second is to get feedback from your customer base – via everything from pop up shops to business pitching events - and don't assume that what worked for your brand at home will work in another country.

The third is that where English is a common language, the power of social media and an e-commerce platform enables you to tap into new territories without any 'boots on the ground' in the early stages. This being said, I don't think there is anything better than immersing yourself into the location and lives of your target audience.

This year I have spent a lot of time in London, and this has really opened my eyes to a different way of doing business and living life. By attending professional networking events and observing my target audience as they go through their working days – from pre-work work-outs to drinks with their team on a Thursday evening – I have learned a huge amount.

I will use this to adapt and improve our strategy for kay me in the UK, as well as cherry picking some of the areas that I most admire - efficient communications, prioritising team bonding time and regarding even leisure time as an opportunity to network - and see if they can be incorporated into the DNA of kay me's company culture back in Japan.

My top tips to anyone looking to launch their business into a new territory are: use your common sense; listen to everything and everybody's opinions, but also work with local experts; see the reality for yourself; be humble – you cannot know everything about a country you have only visited on holiday a few times; learn to localise your brand.

Lessons Learnt

Since launching kay me, one of my biggest challenges has been the transition from a business-to-business (b2b) to a business-to-consumer (b2c) organisation. In particular, I have found communicating, promoting and positioning my brand to a consumer rather than business audience to be a key learning.

For example, during kay me's first two years, stylists for newsreaders would often buy kay me to be worn on-screen. Soon after, we were approached by many stylists requesting dresses for TV drama roles.

The roles were varied, with some being a good fit for the brand, however, most did not reflect kay me customers who are hardworking businesswomen, often juggling multiple demands simultaneously. Upon reflection, we decided to be much more selective when working with TV production companies as their characters and viewers were not always representative of the kay me customer.

From this I learnt the importance of consistently reflecting your brand's message across all platforms and to ensure everybody at kay me understands the core messages at the heart of the brand. This continues to be an area for further growth for kay me, but I see this as an exciting challenge, rather than a daunting prospect.

It is also imperative that you have a financial safety net in place. Often people ask me how I was able to get kay me up and running in such a short space of time and without any major financial backing. The answer is that throughout my career I was always mindful of having reserve funds for when I finally branched out on my own.

Between 2008 and 2011, I managed to save most of my earnings from consulting for future investment. I knew that the consulting role was just a platform for something bigger, something greater, so it made sense to put something aside for the day when that came. The moment kay me launched, however, the bills started to come in thick and fast!

Another important lesson I've learnt during my career is that anything really is possible and a positive learning can come out of difficult life experiences. All experiences, good or bad shape us and I would like to think looking back, my teenage friend would be proud of all my achievements and how much I've grown in confidence since we were 18.

Networking is also incredibly important. Without established on and off line networks in place, I would have really struggled to establish kay me as quickly and as successfully as I did. I have been lucky in that I've always admired my bosses and colleagues as they were very smart and always focused, and it has been a pleasure for me to keep in contact with them.
As a team leader now myself, I strive to inspire other young people in a similar way and as a result have established complementary English-for-business classes for all employees. Not only does this help them engage with customers traveling from overseas, but it also enables them to develop both professionally and personally, as language skills will be useful for the rest of their lives.

A piece of advice I would give particularly to younger readers is to travel. See the world. Have adventures. I really regret not traveling more when I was younger, as when I did start traveling abroad, I realised that I learnt so much about myself by meeting others who culturally were so different from me.
As I have expanded kay me internationally, I've also encountered a big learning curve in communicating with people in different languages.

Finally, I created kay me for businesswomen so that they could look and feel great and with this in mind, my final piece of advice is that as women, we should be strong, proud and not be fearful to share our opinions with others. My voice is often soft but the words I say are strong. After all, women having opinions is a wonderful thing and can only benefit us all.

By Junko Kemi

About The Author

Junko Kemi began her career as a salesperson for one of Japan's leading educational service providers, Benesse. From there, she worked as a marketing consultant for PwC and Boston Consulting Group.

In these roles, she developed a passion for sales and providing cost effective solutions for corporate institutions. It was during this time that the foundations for the concept of kay me were born as she began to feel the need for a better mix of professional attire that could also be appropriate for after-work wear, entertaining clients or eating out with colleagues.

After launching in 2011, kay me how has five Japanese locations (a flagship store in Ginza, a store in downtown Osaka, another at Haneda international airport and concessions in two Tokyo department stores). Junko also launched kay me in London in the summer 2016.

Successful Women In Business – Leadership Edition

To Find Out More Visit:

Website: https://www.kayme.co.uk

Twitter: @kaymetokyo

Instagram: @kaymetokyo

Facebook: kaymelondon

How Self-Discovery Creates Business Success

Your Whole Self:

Sometimes you meet someone and like them or connect with them straight away. Maybe it's their energy, or they tell you about something they like to do or something that they like or don't like. These pieces of information help you look for ways that you are alike and connect with that person. And it's just the same for customers when they come across your business. The way that you present yourself in your business is in every piece of your business. Your brand, your company name, and the service you deliver, your company values, your humour, introversion or extroversion and your confidence.

Let's think about how Oprah does this. She comes across as friendly, approachable, someone that enjoys comfort, a woman on a lifetime quest of self-development, a person that enjoys helping others and is an inclusive person.

Oprah's Core Values Are:

- Staying focused on the present.
- Being strong in her area of self-worth.
- Having a deep sense of purpose.
- Deeply trusting herself.
- Staying connected to nature.
- Maintaining balance in every facet of life.
- Creating space for mindfulness and thought.

The other thing that Oprah does very well is shows her vulnerability and her fans love her for it. She came from a poor background and has had many personal struggles in her life, which she has overcome to achieve great success. The reason Oprah has been able to be her full true self is through personal development, of which one aspect is self-discovery. Self-discovery means exploring different aspects of yourself, looking inside yourself and deeply connecting with yourself. Doing this work will change your life. Let's look at how.

We are multi-dimensional beings. Much like the ecosystem of the natural world, the parts of ourselves all work together to make up our 'whole self'. The ultimate way of being is harmony and balance, in all aspects of our 'self'. This can be hard to achieve with the demands of the modern world, but a good start is to have awareness of these selves and to understand which is in, or out of balance. Doing some self-development in the areas that need attention can make a huge difference to you in terms of how you feel, your energy, your productivity and your success.

Try This Exercise:

Take a sheet of paper and make a list of 'parts' of yourself. Some ideas are the topics below that we are going to explore below; self-confidence, self-worth, self-image, purposeful self, connected self, creative self, resilient self, self-care, self-talk, self-development, spiritual development, empowered self, authentic self.

For each, make a note of how well you think you are achieving each area on a scale of 1-10 (1 is low and 10 is high). You will immediately see where you are out of balance and the guidance below will give you some ideas on rebalancing yourself.

Self-Confidence:

Many people have a sense consciously or unconsciously of not being 'good enough'. This means that they hold back, don't speak up and doubt their own abilities. This can be a problem in life, but the spotlight really shines on it in business. Imagine seeing a speaking opportunity that is a perfect fit for you and gives you the opportunity to speak to your dream customers. But you don't go for it because you think you won't be any good at it, or might make a mistake. Self-discovery will help you build your confidence so that you can go for exciting opportunities and not fear being seen or heard. It's hard to say what affects each person's confidence, but often there are experiences in the past that need to be healed to make the shift to feeling confident.

Once the healing is done, for many people it's like a switch has been turned on and they feel more confident right away. For others, they do the healing and processing and then build up with small steps for instance, by writing a blog, speaking on a podcast, doing a live video, and then speaking at an event.

Try This Exercise:

Draw two vertical columns on a piece of paper. On the left write things you would like to do to make an impact or grow your business. On the right capture what is stopping you. When you read the things on the right think, about how your feelings about yourself affect you taking action. Congratulate yourself on identifying these blocks as that is the first step in shifting them.

Self-Worth :

There's a reason that L'Oreal use 'Because I'm worth it' as their advertising slogan. Everyone wants to feel this way, but most people in some way, will have a chink in their armour.

How it shows up in business is interesting. It might be through pricing where you undercharge because deep down you have feelings that your work is not good enough, someone might object if you charge more, or you won't get any customers at a higher rate. Or it might be a case of imposter syndrome where the night before you are due to deliver a workshop you toss and turn. You worry that you will be rubbish and people will think you don't know what you are doing.

For many people with low self-worth, they find themselves often feeling taken advantage of, overworking, or ending up the one doing the 'dirty work'. This is because they have not been able to say, "No", and this is often referred to as boundary setting.

So how do you go about increasing your self-worth? Through another element of self-discovery which is self-awareness. By being aware of how you feel about things and react to things you can spot triggers and create new behaviours that increase your self-worth. This is fantastic because with each step forward, you get the reward of knowing that you did something for you which feels great and motivates you to do it more.

Try This Exercise:

The next time you feel yourself about to say, "Yes" when you really want to say, "No", try saying one of these things instead:

- "No thank you, I won't be able to".
- "Thank you for asking me, but I can't make that work with my other commitments".
- "As much as I would like to help, I'm currently focusing on some other priorities".
- Or if you need a little more time to decide, try "Let me think about it and I will get back to you".

Self-Image:

As much as the way you think about yourself, the way you present yourself is also important in business. You can choose the image that you want to present but the more congruent it is with the essence of yourself, the more powerful it will be.

Think about the importance of this for major brands and celebrities. Let's take Disney as an example. The Disney princesses all have a look, and a character. If you meet them in the Disney Park, they look exactly like they did in the film, have the mannerisms and act like the character. It all feels aligned (and makes a lot of people happy and adds to Disney's success).

Try This Exercise:

Ask yourself these questions about your own personal image:
Does your image reflect who you are?
How are you expressing your personality in your image?
How are you perceived by others when you first meet them?
Do you like that your clothing expresses your personal style?
Is there anything that you would like to change?
If you are feeling brave, ask some honest friends for their perception of your style.

Purposeful Self:

People talk about mind-set as if it's something you must find, buy, or get. The simple truth is that every single day we are all running a mind-set. It's just that it might not be the one that is most helpful to us!

Take productivity for example. People have long to do lists and big dreams and then might find themselves scrolling social media all day instead of doing the things on their list. What skills are needed to scroll social media? Patience, curiosity, focus and commitment.

All great skills but just applied in the wrong place! If you were to apply those same skills to the to do list that would have been a productive time.

Mind-set is simply how you choose to apply the greatest gift in the world – your amazing mind. The easiest way to apply your mind-set in business is to have a strong purpose about why you do what you do, this aligns your unconscious mind to that purpose. Find a strong sense of purpose and notice how your mind aligns and helps you achieve it.

Try This Exercise:

Ask yourself, what is the biggest purpose that I am here to fulfil?

Connected Self:

A big part of self-discovery is understanding your personal values. This means exploring words which resonate with who you are and what you believe in. The more you live, act and feel that way, the more others will see that in you to which is important in business as it will draw the best customers to you. When you work in alignment to your values it feels good and when things feel good, that is one kind of business success that we all enjoy.

Try This Exercise:

Think of someone that you admire and identify the qualities that they have that you most like and connect with. Things like honest, intuitive, fun, purposeful, generous, loyal, courageous, inspiring, positive and passionate. Make a list of all the ones that appeal to you and then reduce it to about five that matter the most. Make sure you connect with all the words in your final list. When you look at it, you should feel good and know they are things you and aspire to.

Creative Self:

Self-discovery is a major key to unleashing creativity, because creativity is a deeply personal experience. It is often said that writers and actors become completely absorbed when making a book or a movie. As if they are putting their 'whole self' into it. Self-discovery techniques that help you become more creative are connecting with nature, mindfulness, play, exploring different ways to experience joy, removing energetic blocks and visualisation. Imagine creativity as a deep pool in an enchanted forest just waiting for you to either put your toe in or jump fully in. The pool is always there but you need to remember how to get to it and decide how far in you want to immerse yourself.

Try This Exercise:

Close your eyes and imagine yourself in a museum. Imagine wandering into one of the rooms of that museum and there is a large blank canvas. Now you can put onto that canvas anything you like. What do you imagine putting onto it? What materials do you use? What colours are there? What shapes and symbols? You can repeat this exercise and get different results each time which is testament to your amazing creative self.

Resilient Self:

If there's one place you need resilience, it's in business. Business is an ongoing process of knockbacks and lessons, even on the smoothest path to success. James Dyson (inventor) famously said he built the world's most successful vacuum after a 'few thousand prototypes'. 5.127 prototypes to be exact, of which one was successful. Because of the things we see on the internet, it can be easy to believe that setting up and running a business is easy, can be done in just a few hours a week and we can enjoy great success. This may be true for some, but it can also be an ongoing process of trial and failure and highs and lows.

Try This Exercise:

To increase your own resilience, you might like to think about how well you understand and manage these areas of your own resilience:

- Self-Awareness – being aware of when you are feeling 'less than' and taking action to change it.

- Energy Levels – realising that you need rest and taking it when you need it.

- Emotional Health – understanding that as a human being is it perfectly normal to experience a full range of emotions

- Physical Health – nurturing and moving your body to optimise its performance

- Positive relationships – people need people. It really helps to spend time with people that support and energise you

Self-Care:

Self-care is often talked about but what is it really? In its simplest form, it is deciding to take care of yourself in any way that works best for you. Maybe your computer and files stress you out every day, your self-care activity could be to keep them organised and backed up. Or would meal planning and having a shopping routine help you have more free time and less stress? How about investing some time in organising your diary and making sure you pop some time in each day or week to do something for you. Establish a self-care routine. And of course, clutter is never good for us so spending time each week tidying and organising will always make you feel better. If you live or work in a mess, it can block your energy. There are many other types of self-care like exercise, health and beauty, reading and spending time in nature. Whatever it is really doesn't matter.

The most important thing is valuing yourself enough to take care of you, so you feel good and have enough energy to live your life.

Try This Exercise:

Make a list of self-care activities that you could do in certain amounts of time, i.e., 5, 15, 30 and 60 minutes. Schedule time in your diary to do some of those things. Make them non-negotiable and notice the double 'feel good impact' of honouring the commitment to yourself by doing them and enjoying the activity.

Self-Talk:

Self-talk is the narrative that takes place in your mind a lot of the time. The unconscious part of your mind (the greater part of your mind), does not know the difference between fact and fiction. By changing any negative self-talk that you have, you can make an enormous difference to how you feel. Imagine if you had someone in your house or next to you while you work all day saying, 'You're not very good, are you', 'You can't do it' or even 'You're stupid'. It wouldn't be very nice, would it?

Give yourself a break and some kindness and talk to yourself in a more positive way. This is the most powerful way to change your life and your business.

Try This Exercise:

Take a moment now to think of something big that you would like to achieve. Make a note of what thoughts come into your mind as you think about that thing. Are there thoughts that say it's too difficult? That you can't do it. That you're not good enough, don't have time, don't have the skills or will fail. Or are the thoughts all positive? Whatever you notice, that is self-talk. Make sure you finish this exercise by giving yourself some positive messages such as things you know you have done and succeeded at and the skills that made this possible, i.e., you are determined because you met that deadline/completed that task/supported that charity.

Self-Development:

Self-development should be something we all do throughout our lives. We are remarkable and yet many of us never reach our full potential, simply because we don't fully explore all that we are and all that we can be. Self-development is the cornerstone of personal progress and can be done on our own or with the help of experts like coaches, personal trainers, group coaching programmes, attending conferences and joining networks. Self-development is a personal journey but does not need to be taken alone, there is more support than ever available in this area. Good places to start are the self-development bookshelves at Amazon, Ted talks and connecting with others on a similar journey in life or business to yourself.

Try This Exercise:

Make a note of some areas of your life, self, or business that you would like to develop. Then reserve time in your diary on a regular basis and find something you can do in that time that helps you in the area that you want to grow. Maybe find an accountability partner to do this with so you can compare progress and ideas.

Spiritual Self:

At some point in most peoples' lives they will encounter their spiritual self. The degree to which they want to embrace it varies, but for many exploring this aspect opens their mind vastly. Each person's spiritual experience is completely unique which makes it an exciting area. Some people might connect to their spirituality through religion.
Others through meditation, yoga and connecting to nature, amongst many other things. As nature is made up of earth, water, fire, air and space and we are also living with these elements it makes sense that nature is deemed spiritual. Whilst out in nature you might discover a sense of wellbeing and

peace where you could say you are feeling your 'Natural' self. Exploring spirituality is said to help you connect to great health, power, knowledge, wisdom and happiness. Spiritually connected people enjoy deep connection to their innate intuition. Connecting to your spiritual self at any level, can be helpful to your business success as it adds another level to you as a person which is enriching and part of your personal evolution.

Try This Exercise:
Sit or lie quietly. Become aware of your breathing, the temperature of the room and how each arm and leg feels in comparison to the other. Notice yourself becoming still inside. Ask your unconscious mind for a sign, sense, feeling or signal and notice what happens. Connecting to your own unconscious mind is a powerful gateway to all sorts of spiritual adventures.
Empowered Self:

Once you have been on a journey of self-discovery and achieved a better connection with yourself, you can avoid feelings of dread when you give your elevator pitch. Instead, you will know at a deep level who you are in life and in business. You will find it so easy to stand up and say I'm < your name and what you do >. People will feel this certainty and confidence coming from you and your personal power will attract well aligned clients to you. Empowerment means feeling stronger and more confident, more in control and knowing your worth. Self-discovery helps with self-acceptance and any blocks there might be to feel truly empowered.

Try This Exercise:

Stand in front of the mirror, in an upright position with your hands on your hips. Say the words 'I am' followed by a statement that makes you feel empowered. Try different ones until you find one or more that you truly connect with and makes you feel empowered.

Here Are Some To Try. 'I Am':

- A strong person
- Independent
- Worthy
- Empowered
- Open to possibility

Authentic Self:

So many people struggle with understanding themselves, liking themselves, accepting themselves and knowing who they are. By investing in your own personal development in the form of self-discovery, you will be able to have a strong sense of yourself, discover your true essence of self and realise your own personal power. Self-discovery can't help but create business success, because ultimately business is about relationships. By developing a deeper relationship with yourself and appreciating your uniqueness, you'll feel free to be your true self.

Try This Exercise:

Write a personal statement that captures your essence. So that someone who had never met you could read it and get a true sense of who you are. Then repeat the exercise but for your business.

Know Yourself To Grow Yourself

By understanding these different aspects of yourself, you can really create a strong alignment of your 'Self' and realise more of your own magic. You'll embrace places, people and things that make you feel most alive to fully enjoy your truest self. Continue your own journey of self as it's a continuous process which allows you to evolve and grow.

You'll find as you become each new version of yourself, that you may have healing work to do. It might sound strange to think that healing yourself is part of your business journey, but everything starts with you, including your business. Every limiting belief that you break through allows you to move forward more easily in your business. You will find that your self-development is also your business development.

Your emotional, physical and spiritual health as a huge part of your business success. Investing in your own self-discovery will pay off in so many ways for you, including your business success.

By Honey Lansdowne

About The Author

I've always been fascinated by the mind and did my first emotional intelligence course in 1999! I'm qualified in many things including NLP, coaching, counselling, mental health, nutrition, energy, hypnosis, RTT, mindfulness and tapping. I use them in an intuitive way, to suit what my client needs. I love working with the unconscious mind. It is the true gateway to making changes and life changing insights. The common denominator in my work is always helping people to feel and be better. I work with women worldwide online and my specialism is helping women build confidence and self-esteem through self-discovery. This means healing thoughts, beliefs, behaviours and experiences that cause feelings of not being 'Good Enough'.

This is true life changing self-development which builds confidence, personal power, and happiness. Everyone deserves the chance to see the value of their true, unique and magical self.

What I Offer:

- Transformational Coaching to connect you to your truest self
- Healing Hypnotherapy to help with anxiety and depression
- Rapid Transformational Therapy to heal your inner child, remove blocks, limiting beliefs and unhelpful thought patterns
- Hypnosis training to become an amazing hypnotherapist
- A wide range of online products, courses and hypnosis downloads.
- Free online coaching for women once a month
- Free online anxiety relief course
- Free online depression relief course
- Free online confidence course

To Find Out More Visit:

Website: honeylansdowne.co.uk

Facebook: https://www.facebook.com/www.honeylansdowne.co.uk/

Instagram: https://www.instagram.com/honeylansdowne/

Twitter: hlhypnotherapy

Successful Women In Business – Leadership Edition

Self-Doubt to Self-Accomplishment
Lorena Öberg's Story

LIke most successful people, the seeds of who I am today started in early childhood. Being born into a highly dysfunctional middle class family has shaped the very nature of who I am and how I live my life today.

My mother handed me over to my nanny as soon as she brought me back from the hospital. My nanny Dina, as we know her to this day, took on full parenting roles. It was Nanny Dina who did the school runs, made sure my homework was done and who took me to doctor's appointments. Still, this part of my early life was quite happy and stable. We lived with my maternal grandmother and my father, who by this time divorced from my mother, visited daily. The seeds to my self-esteem were sewn during this time and I credit this early stability and unconditional love for much of my success.

This all changed at the age of 8. My mother, for reasons that are still a mystery, decided to move the family to the city where my oldest sister lived. She unceremoniously fired my beloved nanny and put my grandmother in a nursing home leaving in her wake the lives of those that had served her for so many years. My father was devastated although he lost no time taking refuge in the arms of various unsavoury women soon forgetting both his sorrows and sadly mine.

My mother's new life was a disaster. It was the first time I'd lived with my oldest sister, 22 years my senior. My sister was 30 and, like my mother, took a liking to married men. At such an early age I could never have realised that my sister had been abandoned in a boarding school at the age of 5 and mother never visited. Like me, my sister was a very much unwanted child. Mother was 15 when she had her and was in her late thirties when I arrived. My sister unconsciously thought that I was my mother's favourite and of course, my mother wasted no time in playing us off against each other. I absolutely stood no chance against this grown woman who took huge gratification in seeing tears rolling down my eyes. The entire time my mother looked on with delight, she had found the perfect puppet to do her dirty work.

My daily needs where nowhere, on the scale of my mother's list of priorities, her main priority was her married lover and her second was travelling. If I dared to ask for clothes to replace the ones I had grown out of, I would be told that I was too fat and that if I lost weight they would fit me. If I needed money for school supplies, I was made to grovel after a telling off for not making my pencils last longer. The message I was sent was clear "You're an inconvenience in my life".

I went to University at 24, partly because I didn't have a job that paid well enough until then and partly because years of being told I was stupid and lazy had taken a toll of how I viewed myself. Everything I had ever tried to do had been sabotaged.

I funded my studies by working full time. Once at university, I went to lectures during the week and worked ten-hour shifts on Friday, Saturday and Sunday. But it wasn't long, before I began to do well. This was a revelation because I believed I was stupid. Soon, I was in the honour roll and for the first time in my life I had the respect of my peers. I put myself through all sorts of self-tests trying to convince myself that I was actually intelligent. By the time I graduated, I had finally proven my family wrong. I was intelligent and capable of anything. From then on, no one would be able to make me believe differently.

Although my self-esteem would never again be compromised, my boundaries were another story. I had very low expectations of how people should treat me. I had been raised in an environment where promises were not kept and questions were met with conflict. In short, I had learnt to expect NOTHING from ANYONE. I figured out that true happiness comes from within, and in my case happiness came from living my life in a way I thought was honourable. I tried to do what I believed to be right and live my life with what I now know is called integrity.

Sadly, low self-worth had landed me in a marriage with a man with traits very much like my mother. I have to admit that this didn't bother me very much as I had the coping mechanisms to deal with drama and everything being blamed on me. For years I was happy, and even more so when my two wonderful children were born. I understood that to keep the peace in my marriage, just as I had done growing up, I had to have no expectations of anything.

I worked full time to pay the bills and to give my children everything they needed. My husband just paid the mortgage and only the mortgage. This is what he said married couples did, and to be honest, it was not worth the argument so I complied. Staying quiet during conflict seemed to be my only defence. I never saw my girlfriends because for me to go out was not worth the backlash when I got home. Although he didn't do much to help with the children he was and is a good father. He played with them and indulged their every whim. The children would talk AT him for hours well beyond the point where most parents would scream SILENCE! Yet he had and still has the patience of a saint!

The marriage, infidelities, lies, and the constant struggle of having all of the responsibilities, financial and otherwise, were wearing me down. Being with a controlling man, who would start an argument if I took too long to wash my hair and whose spending was out of control, left me feeling trapped. But it wasn't until I saw him trying to manipulate my 6 year old daughter that I was compelled to start making a change.

I went online to try to figure out what to do. Amongst my many searches and vast research, I came across a condition known as Narcissistic Personality Disorder. Suddenly there was an explanation for everyone and everything throughout my entire life. The pattern of abuse, the infidelities, the self-serving behaviours, the lies and being blamed for everything, it finally all made sense. The more I researched the subject the more I saw the pieces of the puzzle fit together. It was then I realised that my situation could never get better, that the people around me would never change and that the only person who can change my children's future, and mine, was me.

The final straw came after an altercation between us, which took place in front of friends, and the next day when I came home from work I found him sulking trying to spin the incident to be my fault. I had no more fight left in me; he had taken every last bit of energy I had to keep our marriage together and to try to give our children a happy home. Instead of trying to appease him, this time, I asked him to leave and this time there was no turning back. I wanted a divorce and there would be no reconciliation, or any promises of another a holiday. This time, it was over, in my heart, in my soul, it was over. He soon left declaring that he was getting nothing from our marriage and that no one would ever want me. I was past the point of caring who wanted me, my only focus was providing a good life for my children. Then from the moment he walked out that door I began my detox.

Anyone that was not contributing in a positive way to my life had to go. My last conversation with my sister had been years before when she put the phone down on me declaring that she would never speak to me again. In my heart, I had always left that door open in case one day, she wanted to resume contact. But this time, I closed that door for good.

I have to admit that when my husband left I felt a huge amount of relief. Whilst we were together I had been as good a single mother the entire time, but now without the constant stress of possible conflict, it was bliss. We had agreed verbally how assets were going to be split so that the children could stay in the family home. We had agreed to wait for two years before filing for divorce and that he would continue to pay for the mortgage, this happened for only a few months. Soon I began to get letters telling me the mortgage wasn't being paid and that he had used our home as security to take out large loans. It became apparent to me that he was trying to bankrupt me and ruin my credit, I had no choice but to proceed with filing for divorce.

His revenge came after the children wanted to spend a week with him and a week with me. This arrangement can work very well when both parents are doing it for the interest of the children, but I knew this wouldn't be the case. I had evidence to prove he was doing it to leverage a better financial settlement out of me and to pay less child support. I knew beyond a shadow of a doubt that if I had full custody of the children, they would grow up to have a close relationship with both parents. But I knew him, if he had them half the time, they could be used as pawns in our divorce.

I found myself faced with a high court battle and no money to cover solicitor fees. So I did the only thing that I could do, I quit my job, and went on government benefits, got ready to lose the only home my children had ever known, all to make fighting for my children my full time job. I was confident that I had right on my side, I self-represented. I would show up to court on my own to face him and his barrister, and believed I would come out of that courtroom with what I wanted and what was fair for my children and I, because I had right on my side.

The fight went on for three and a half years, and it was during this time that I had to come up with a way of supporting my children. I needed to find something I could do around my children and their routines, especially as they were so little, only 5 and 7. The thought of living from government funds and raising my children in that way terrified me but with my husband dragging out the divorce, it was difficult to say the least. Then one day a doctor friend of mine said to me "why don't you try tattoo removal, you'd be good at that". They turned out to be the most prophetic words any person has ever said to me.

I immediately began researching tattoo removal and the numbers stacked up. I found Dermace Training Academy near Leeds, so I took the plunge. I also trained in Medical and Cosmetic Tattooing at the same time, and put it all on credit cards. At that point in my life I thought I would have to file for bankruptcy, so I figured I may as well have a new career from it. I never did have to file for bankruptcy and my gut instinct was right about my new career.

I then made it my mission to be successful, I got busy writing a business plan and making a website. I made a website myself because I had no money to hire anyone. I also knew a bit about ranking on Google and SEO (search engine optimisation) so I put all my skills into action. Still, I was broke, and without any money I couldn't rent a premises and without a premises, I didn't have a business. I heard through the grapevine that a local hair salon had a beauty room to rent. I immediately went to speak to the owner, and used money from my credit cards to put down my first deposit. That day I remember with great fondness, not only was that the beginning of my business but it was the day I met my now husband.

So I began my self-employed journey but with no money to advertise, business was slow. I advertised in all the free places I could and prayed that someone would see it. Early on I told myself that I had a full time job. If I wasn't treating someone, I was working on marketing. One such day, I was home working on marketing with the television on in the background and it came to me, *"If lasers worked like this, and micro-needling worked like that….if I used them together in this way….wouldn't that work for stretch marks?"*

At that time, my body was covered in stretch marks. I pulled out my equipment, used a lot of numbing cream and away I went. I nearly fainted a few times but I completed my treatment, and a month later my stretch marks were greatly reduced. I then called all my friends to trial it on them; they all had great results too. I knew I had something special, and so, **DermaEraze** was born.

I had a couple of bespoke treatments to offer. I had tattoo removal, permanent makeup and stretch marks as specialist treatments under my belt. The problem was that no one knew about me and with no money to advertise I thought I was doomed. The salon owner didn't allow me to put anything in the window so walk through trade was out of the question but my website was ranking a bit better. Until one day I received a phone call from a journalist who was writing an article about stretch mark treatments and asked if she could come try my treatment and write about it. She wrote a very honest article, and despite of her complaints about how much it hurt, she told the truth, and how it worked.

I was working between school runs, an irregular client flow and struggling to pay the rent for the treatment room. Stefan, my now husband pointed out the financial difficulties in all sorts of graphs, which I could barely see through my tears. I knew that if I didn't do well, I wouldn't be able to feed my kids, and if I did well, my ex-husband would try to go after my business. He had already tried to ruin my credit and make us homeless, so at this point nothing would have surprised me.

One day I received a phone call from Groupon asking if I wanted to run a deal for Permanent Makeup. The numbers didn't make sense and so I declined. Then I asked them if they would run a deal on stretchmark's. We went through the numbers and we were able to come up with a deal that made sense. The deal ran and we sold 175 Groupons. Overnight, I was solid with clients for eight hours a day! Some upgraded to larger areas some didn't but it didn't matter because I was getting my name out there. Soon Wowcher contacted me and we did the same. These relationships lasted years and although my business is now at a point where we no longer run deals, I will forever be grateful to those two companies. They did the marketing for me at a point when I simply could not afford to advertise. My advice to anyone who believes these companies charge too much in commission is to negotiate and structure the proposed deals to accommodate both parties' interests.

I soon realised that putting all my eggs in the daily deal basket was dangerous and I wanted to stand out and promote my treatments through the press so I took on a PR agency. I showed them that article about

Successful Women In Business – Leadership Edition

DermaEraze and told them I had something really special, we agreed on a fee that I could afford and got started with PR.
Taking on PR was a huge leap of faith. I remember asking if they really thought I would get press coverage. My self-doubt was fuelled by the ghosts of my past telling me that I was useless, stupid and incapable of ever succeeding. My PR sensed this and the next day in the post was a book called "The Secret". When I received it I thought it was a business book when I read it I realised it was so much more. That book taught me how to stop self-sabotaging. It taught me to change my thought pattern from self-doubt to empowerment. It didn't happen overnight but I began my internal detox. The first step was to, again, get rid of the toxic people in my life, but the most important step was to get rid of what they left behind. I will always be a product of my up-bringing but today I choose to only hold on to the parts that make me extraordinary.
My PR told me I needed an address in London, preferably Harley Street, I told them they were crazy and I could barely afford the premises I had. Still, something clicked and I grabbed my kids and went off to Harley Street, walking into 1 Harley Street and asked them if they rented rooms by the hour. They said they did, and so, we got busy booking in my first press days. From those press days, I began to get busy in London and six months later I had to take full time residence at number 1 Harley Street. I'm still there and am still very happy.
During this time I was doing something I had no idea about it was so pioneering in the beauty and cosmetics industry. When my clients came in for Permanent Makeup, often they would come in with old work that I couldn't tattoo over. I would suggest to my clients that I laser off their old work and start fresh. In the beginning I relied on test patching, figuring out how different pigments reacted under the laser and reading as many medical journals as I could get my hands on. I am fully insured to work on the face so it never occurred to me that it couldn't be done.
One day someone added me to a Facebook group for Permanent Makeup Artists. I lurked for a while because by this time I had been in the beauty industry for two years and had worked in a very insular way so knew no one from the industry.
At first I was very reluctant to fraternise with my "competitors". What I saw was that my colleagues were posting photos of people with bad work, saying that they were "disfigured for life", and the whole time I was thinking *"are*

you kidding me, put her under my laser and I'll have her good to go in three treatments".
By the time anyone told me that lasers didn't work on removing permanent makeup, I had been successfully doing it for years. I remember responding to a photo about this that was posted in one of the groups so I replied with series of ten before and after photos. I had been using custom made lasers. This is when people really started to take notice. I began to get messages asking if I could train people. I dismissed this at first but after the tenth message I thought, I can do this and so I did.
I was soon asked to speak at a large conference. After that, other conferences followed and soon, somehow, I became the go to person for the removal of permanent makeup. What I didn't realise, in that little room inside a hair salon, was that I was doing something that no one else thought possible within the industry. I didn't know it couldn't be done, so I just did it.
I soon got asked to speak at a Permanent Makeup Conference, and then another and another. I began to get asked to teach in America and so my lasers had to go through all the legal hoops there. I now teach all over the world and speak to hundreds of people about removing pigment from the face safely.
Today, my husband and I run two very busy clinics. Celebrities seek me out for my skin rejuvenation and other bespoke treatments. People travel from all over the world to have treatments with us and DermaEraze is being rolled out to clinics worldwide allowing women from all over to benefit from it. I am in high demand for speaking and teaching across the globe. To this day I am still so taken back when I get asked to speak at conferences and pass on my advice. People are interested in what I have to say and wish to learn from me. However, this is not what makes me successful.
True success can only be achieved when one reaches a point in their lives where they are happy. Any child of abuse will tell you that the one thing we want above everything else is a loving family. My divorce is long over and the children are still close to their father. Three years ago Stefan and I got married on the day that was my mother and father in law's 50th wedding anniversary. In the same little medieval church they walked down the aisle 50 years earlier.

Successful Women In Business – Leadership Edition

My mother and father in law are the parents I never had who love and respect me and dote on our children. When I'm on television or I win an award, it's my mother in law that calls to congratulate me.

They are the ones that fly in to help us with the children during school holidays. Through them I have learnt that the only thing that is thicker than water is love.

I now live a life without drama. No huge ups or downs. No one uses guilt to control me. My children taught me that in order for them to be happy, I have to be happy first. I have achieved my goals and desires to make sure they did not have the life I'd broken free from.

Life is good, not because I'm jet-setting around the world but because when I come home, I do so to a loving family. I come home to giggles, happy children and a husband that appreciates the life we have together, a real man who loves my children like his own, and in laws that mean the world to me.

By Lorena Öberg

About The Author

Lorena Öberg is a world-renowned Skin Repair Expert, CEO and Founder of Lorena Öberg Skincare. Based in London's prestigious Harley Street and Surrey, Lorena offers patients specialist treatments for various skin conditions using pioneering techniques, including tattoo removal, semi-permanent make up correction and migration.

Lorena is also a pioneer in scar and stretch mark reduction and recently launched DermaEraze®, a unique technique that has been hailed in international press for its high success rates. Under her brand DermaLipo® Lorena also offers a highly acclaimed advanced body contouring, non-invasive ultrasonic liposuction, ultrasound inch-loss and skin tightening treatment, with proven results.

Lorena runs an international training academy where she uses her skills and abilities to teach the next generation. She regularly attends conferences and lectures across the globe and speaks about various topics ranging from industry trends, motivation, regulations and new techniques.

Successful Women In Business – Leadership Edition

Lorena founded her successful business five years ago with £100 and having two young children to support. Lorena first discovered her talent after a friend suggested she tried tattoo removal. With a change in career she has never looked back. In 2013 Lorena married Stefan Öberg and the couple live in Caterham Surrey with their family.

To Find Out More About Lorena Öberg Skincare And Treatments Visit:

www.lorenaoberg.co.uk

Menopausitivity

Life begins at 40. Well I'm not sure about that but a massive shift in my life certainly began then. Although, I didn't realise it at the time. I had reached my career goal, spanning 24 years in the corporate jungle. I had fulfilled a personal goal, to travel around Australia. I was happily married. Until I wasn't... It took less than 3 years for my marriage to begin to disintegrate. I lost multiple jobs back to back. I lost my home. I was broken. And ultimately in December 2020 I was ready to give up on life entirely. Yet here I am a year later and I'm happier than I've ever been!

How Did This Happen?
Opportunity, decision and believe it or not - menopause! Although it may have been menopause that broke me initially - it was most definitely also the making of me. Here is my journey turning my 'menopause meltdown' into my 'menopause mission'.

So Where Did It All Start?
It's 2014. I'd just lost my job - due to having excessive time off for mental health related issues. This in itself was damaging enough as I have always been successful in my career, focused, dedicated and results driven. I had been used to high level positions with high profile businesses, good salary and massive potential. But I was now struggling to keep a job of the most basic nature. I'd been forced into a different, less demanding career due to relocating with my hubby. Focus, organisational skills and short term memory had pretty much escaped me.

Not very helpful in a corporate environment at any level, but at the time I'd written it off to the work challenge not being great enough to incentivise me. Boredom breeds inactivity.

This naturally put a strain on the marriage (my husband was the stereotypical 'work a 40 hour week and save every spare penny' kinda guy).

Successful Women In Business – Leadership Edition

I'd been married all of 2 years. On top of this, I was constantly tired and had absolutely no interest in our physical relationship. In fact I'd go to any lengths to avoid it. I was miserable, irritable and lethargic. Not exactly fun to be around. I had also gained almost 3 stone in weight since we got married. We argued constantly, didn't seem to have any common interests left and barely communicated with each other. It's hardly surprising then that we parted ways 2 years later.

Some might say it was a marriage that should never have happened and although I'd now agree with them, menopause definitely had its part to play in the breakdown. This left me in even more turmoil, emotionally, mentally and financially.

However, I battled on, taking medical advice and resigning myself to the fact I was having an extended period of depression - thinking my 'condition' was as a result of the stress of my situation. But the loss of a husband wasn't really the worst part. It was the loss of everything else... My self-worth, my lifestyle (not that it was ever actually lavish), my confidence and my pride.

However, a few months after we split, I was approached by a previous boss who suggested I apply for a new position that was coming up with the company she was with. At the time, I was delighted to have the opportunity to get back into management in an industry I knew well. I thought this would be the solution, given that my previous job had started this mood of depression and melancholy right?

Obviously what I needed was a mental challenge - a job I could get my teeth into. Start feeling like myself again. I thrive when my brain is put to work. I applied and was successful - however, the timing couldn't have been worse. Unbeknownst to me, my menopause symptoms had only just surfaced but were about to get a whole lot worse. The job itself was amazing! Exactly what I had been waiting for. But my brain could no longer cope. My office management skills had all but disappeared. I had brain fog, couldn't focus, couldn't organise or plan anything - all of the things I'd been known for in previous jobs. I could not comprehend what was happening. I simply couldn't operate at the high level required for the role. I was devastated, frustrated and totally embarrassed. This then led to further depression and anxiety. Which led to time off. Which led to me losing one of the best jobs I've ever had.

The shame was immense. I couldn't explain my 'illness' other than it was depression related along with never ending fatigue. If I'd been my boss, I'd have fired me too. I sounded so pathetic and felt even more so. But once I'd been let go, I had stopped caring. About everything. I was by now living in a friend's flat on a very low rent, unemployed, on benefits and avoiding ALL social interaction.

After a few months, I was beyond struggling with money. I had to tell my friend the rent was going to be late by a couple of weeks. This did not go down well and she threatened to throw me out. I had nowhere else to go, and couldn't afford it even if I did. So I made the decision to leave Aberdeen. My only option was to rent a single room in the house of a complete stranger. I couldn't believe this was my life - 46 years old with absolute nothing to show for it. But thankfully, we actually became good friends. It could have been a horrific experience otherwise.

This low actually helped though, I was determined it was not going to be my long term situation. Over the next 6 months I tried to rebuild my life by starting my own pet sitting business. Minimal overheads and a true love of animals - best job ever right? I also had a network marketing business that I'd played with on and off over the years. I resurrected that as it was something I could do no matter where about in the country I was when on pet sitting jobs. But no matter how determined I seemed to be, I still struggled to do either the job effectively enough to earn decent money.

During some routine tests (as I have hypothyroidism), it was revealed that I was most likely hitting peri-menopause. However, a global shortage of HRT (Hormone Replacement Therapy) meant I was unable to get the correct treatment. The diagnosis had at least gone some way to explain my ever increasing symptoms but there didn't appear to be a solution. I seemed destined to be stuck in this one room, feeling low, losing self-belief and watching my dreams fade away.

Successful Women In Business – Leadership Edition

During the summer of that year, my mum had been to visit me and we made the decision to find somewhere we could share together. Approaching 47, I certainly hadn't planned to 'move in with Mum' ever again. But, it was an opportunity to better our individual living situations and very much the sensible choice at that time. So we pooled our resources and moved into a gorgeous 3 bedroomed house in October 2019. This felt like a fresh start. Surely this was when my life was going to change. My pet business was now doing quite well and my financial situation was improving. I even had a proper office space in our house. I'd taken steps to improve my mind-set through meditation and manifesting. Things I'd 'tried' previously but with no real conviction. But this time I was absolutely positive my life was about to soar.

Everything was going great until the following year... My menopause symptoms had worsened, in particular the irritability and depression. To such a point that on Christmas Eve, I'd had enough of life. I actually didn't want to wake up on Christmas Day or any day after. It seemed to creep up on me in the blink of an eye. One minute I was prepping for the Christmas meal and watching cheesy movies, the next it felt like a switch had been turned off. I was angry about everything, yet nothing. I had a huge argument with Mum about a very minor situation. I felt so useless and unnecessary, everything felt pointless. Given how hard I'd been working to grow my business and get consistent with mind-set, this came as an immense shock. So here I was now 47, living with my Mum, broke financially and broken emotionally. I truly don't think I could ever feel any lower.

But when you *are* at the lowest of lows, there's only one way to go back up. Somehow I battled through, knowing deep down - nothing else was really an option. And the level of guilt I felt for how I'd treated Mum was unbearable. However, by the end of January although I was still struggling, somehow now I actually had some semblance of a will to live. I went back to the GP to discuss my depression, anxiety and fatigue as I wasn't prepared to feel this way anymore. I also spoke to them about the menopause again. Further blood tests were done but finally, after they reconfirmed I was showing signs 'highly indicative' of menopause. This time around, HRT had become more readily available so I bit their hand off to be prescribed it.

At Last - This Was The Turning Point
Once I'd realised I had in fact actually been fighting with massive hormonal imbalances for around 5 years, I started to blame myself less, give myself less of a hard time. It really wasn't my fault. Then it all started to fall into place. The medication was kicking in. My mood was lifting, I was regaining control of my mind and I was getting through the fog. Around mid-February, possibly *the* most random thing happened that was set to determine the next part of my journey. Out of the blue I was messaged by a Facebook friend, one I'd never actually spoken to before. She was excited about an online event that was coming up. When I asked her what it was, I swear her answer struck me like lightning. And here's why...

I had come to realise I'd likely never work for anyone else again. My ongoing symptoms were definitely not conducive to a corporate job. My existing businesses were doing ok but not as well as I really wanted. So in my quest for additional income, I had been toying with a new project. From my 8 or so years in and out of network marketing, I'd built up a ton of knowledge and skills around social media.

I knew I had enough in my head to put together a course to help others use social media effectively. I just didn't know how...

And what was this online event? A Masterclass on how to build your own online course. I hadn't even told anyone about my new idea, certainly hadn't mentioned it anywhere online. Now you see why that message felt like a sign?

Here was my opportunity to try something different. Something I could do from home. Something which wouldn't exacerbate my health struggles. I absolutely said yes to that Masterclass. Whilst attending the event, I made a decision - a commitment. 2021 would be *the* year I'd change my life.

I was fed up being fed up. I knew the only person who could really do anything about it was me. I signed up for two further programmes with the same company. I was actually going to become an accredited coach and online course creator. I'd never done either before and although it was a bit scary, the thought of this new career lit a fire in my belly. I had passion, focus and most of all - energy for life. Because I finally felt like I had a purpose - a mission. And here comes my best advice to anyone reading, take every opportunity you're given. Don't over think it, don't worry if you think you can't do something, at least give it a try - you just never know where it will lead you. Because this is where the absolutely life changing stuff can happen. It definitely did for me.

I had found something that totally aligned with me, something I wanted to wake up for - something I knew could genuinely help others. Whilst studying, another lightning bolt happened... Within the first couple of weeks, I had connected with one of my fellow students, to such a point we became convinced we could even be twins in another universe. We're so aligned, we share the same goals, the same ethics and the same desire to provide value to the world. We initially bonded over a love of rock music but this quickly became a much stronger connection and we decided to join forces as a business. We had both been at a similarly low point in our lives at the exact same time, so when we met, it truly felt like fate - we had saved each other. But this would not have happened if I had ignored that fateful opportunity.

We have immense trust we support each other always and are now growing a fabulous business together. If you find someone who truly 'gets you' - hold on tight. It's easy for others to say, 'Just believe in yourself' but it's not always easy to do. However, get someone else who's rooting for you every step of the way and you can climb mountains. That's what we do for each other and we are sharing every part of this journey with each other. It truly is incredible what a difference a year can make. Especially when you focus on your mind-set, find your mission and get committed to it.

Mind-set will mean something different to everyone but in essence, it's finding a way to regain focus. Whatever it is that works for you - do it often until it becomes second nature. And you might not even know what your mission is until it hits you in the face. This is where those opportunities come in. Even if it seems totally different to what you *think* it is, if it's something that tugs at your heart or lights your soul - just do it. If you're over thinking it - it's not your true mission. Once you do find it you'll absolutely know, as it will become such an integral part of your life - your entire reason for being. This mission has given us both determination like never before. We have built our business from absolutely nothing, with minimal expense but a whole lot of love. We're just regular girls, using our life experience to give something back. No special skills required. We just grabbed an opportunity for change and are taking action every day to get closer to our dreams. We invested whatever we had into ourselves, learning new things in order to create a new life. We have been adaptable when those plot twists have arisen. We've been open to feedback and used it to fine tune our niche and evolve our services. It became clear we were very passionate about raising awareness of menopause and this has now become the core of our business. We didn't give up when it didn't succeed overnight. And most importantly - we do something every single day to develop the business. Whether it's talking to new people, learning new skills or giving value to our audience, we are focused on progression. In less than a year we have built an online community, a loyal customer base, a website, online programs and our signature in person retreat. Once you find your true authentic self and your passion, you'll let nothing get in your way. I barely recognise the person I was 12 months ago and at the time, it felt as though I had nothing to live for. Now I'm in the middle of a wonderful new adventure and it's already given me opportunities I couldn't have imagined. I've been featured in multiple press articles, magazines and guested on podcasts. I have a wonderful and worthwhile business and I'm even writing a menopause self-help book full of Menopausitivity.

It still seems surreal to be saying these things as it's a world away from the bad place I was in last year. There's so much more on my vision board and I'm excited for all the ways I'll be helping people in the future. I'm actually grateful for all the hardships that have gone before if even one thing in my past had been different, I wouldn't be in this exact place right now.

And I know it's exactly where I'm supposed to be. Absolutely everything that's happened in your life is for a reason but only if you choose to see it that way...

I was floored by menopause symptoms, they contributed to me facing divorce, multiple job loss and saw me close to being homeless and bankrupt. But those experiences have made me stronger and more determined than ever. Whatever you are dealing with right now - it will get better. The light at the end of the tunnel might seem so far away but it is there. You just have to keep moving forward.

So, go out there and get whatever it is you want - obstacles are simply lessons in becoming the best version of you.

By Debi Wallbank

About The Author

Debi Wallbank is a self-taught entrepreneur. With a background in corporate management, she now co-owns a business which is a source of support, information, education and community for women around the world. One of the business missions is to eliminate the stigma of menopause and enable women to rock their menopausal years.

The business also provides holistic coaching alongside practical skills in social media, personal branding and online business.

Now divorced, Debi shares a house with her retired Mum so they can be of close support to each other. Debi is a keen amateur cook, loves photography and is a self-proclaimed 'crazy cat lady'! She also loves reading, watching movies and of course - writing. Now 48 years old, Debi is focused on becoming a motivational speaker and aims to talk on stage to over 10,000 people before she turns 50.

To Find Out More Visit:

https://heartcorewarriors.co.uk

https://www.instagram.com/menopausewarriorcoach/

https://allmylinks.com/heartcorewarriors

MADE FOR SUCCESS

Discussion about Resilience and Perseverance in Business

The concept of success has an abstract general definition but has a specific meaning to all of us. I, for one, believe that success is personal and cannot be judged from the outside based on ones' achievements. What do I mean by that? Although we can celebrate and clap hands at a person on the stage holding an award and consider them successful, we cannot determine whether their satisfaction is based on this one accomplishment.

Personally, I base my success on the balance I was able to establish between business and family life. My triumphs and achievements come from being capable to lead flourishing businesses while, at the same time, observing my family dynamics develop and mature into different stages as a result of my growth.

In this chapter I will discuss my journey to success unfolding the opportunities and challenges I have faced throughout the time period I have been an active entrepreneur. Nonetheless, this chapter will unveil methods used in order to build resilience and to persevere in my line of business. Although self-motivation has always been my lead instigator, I have often struggled to discover the inside strength which guides me in pursuing my development as an entrepreneur. Being able to lead four companies, (which includes hosting a popular podcast), along with being a mother of four, means that my journey to success has not always been smooth and sleeky. There have been sacrifices, threats, ups and downs and I was often challenged by outside influences which I had no leverage and control over. Yes, starting your own business means being your own boss, giving you the freedom of choice of when you work, how you work and what you work on, but it is also very demanding, time consuming and at times very stressful.

Creating a business does brings about flexibility and a sense of control. You can control the initial functions of the business and build on its place value in the market in which it operates and thrives. Of course, whilst being in business, you still must cater to market demand, but you choose how to do that and having this freedom gives you greater autonomy. It is true that launching a small business should never be undermined as no small venture. For return of investment, you will pay for it in sweat, all the while working hard to move upwards. But in my experience that is okay because entrepreneurs don't fold from effort or retreat because of tough challenges that may lie ahead. We aim to do big things, so that big things bring greater reward and long-term satisfaction.

Some of the points I have suggested are reasons why I found starting my own business both appealing and satisfying. As you evolve and develop your business, you begin to feel a sense of pride. You can't beat the pleasure of feeling exalted. One other reason why I started my own business is because I wanted to do something that would thrill me. A lot of people dream of work that centers on something they are passionate about. It's an advantage to be able to focus on doing the things that you love, also that you are passionate about and that will pay off.

Some Of My Biggest Interests Are:

- Events Planning & Management
- Public Relations
- Entertainment
- Travel, Leisure & Tourism

I am entirely motivated by operating in industries that connect, that you can manipulate to become a multi-service or later a group, firm or corporation that you can scale up. All my business functions have been beneficial somewhat as I have been able to broaden my networks over time and have accessed a multitude of opportunities as a result. This brings about possibilities for future expansion and a position on the international playing field. I am motivated but also inspired by these possibilities. Becoming my own success story is what it's always been about for me. While pursuing my aspirations in the entrepreneurial world, I have understood the importance of resilience and perseverance and learned that those two-character traits have a crucial influence on my willingness to confront the challenges on my business journey.

Some people have chosen the road to contentment, they enjoy working 9 to 5pm every day, only having their bosses question their performance. And there is absolutely nothing wrong with that, I admire people who are content with having a strict schedule, two holidays a year and live their life comfortably and happily. However, as an entrepreneur, my desire to continuously absorb knowledge and explore opportunities in diverse domains would not allow me to be stuck in the same place, interacting with the same people for a long period of time. I am always willing to broaden my network, to discover more creative perspectives and to apply diverse, innovative ideas into my own work. I can identify with a quote from one of my biggest influencers when relating to the point on staying in the same place...

"If You Opt For A Safe Life, You Will Never Know What It's Like To Win."
Richard Branson, *Screw It, Let's Do It: Lessons In Life*

From a personal point of view, I believe the first step in achieving resilience is ensuring the business plan and the initial idea is of importance to the person pursuing it. Whether it is an issue or a gap in the market they have identified themselves or they are interested and passionate about the area they are wishing to operate in. There will obviously be scope for change and exploration as your plan evolves, this is just a part of the process which will hopefully initiate a robust, concise and tangible business plan.

Working hard and identifying meaning in your own actions is often challenging and the process can develop in a complex procedure which will eventually bring in growth and development.

Surrounding yourself with like-minded people is my second recommendation which can help you build strength and resilience. Like I have previously mentioned, while I admire people who are content with their 9 to 5 jobs, I cannot help but feel envious of their comfort. Thus, participating at networking events and finding individuals with similar interests on social media is highly important. It is a lot more important than I would have envisioned it in the beginning of my journey. Social media platforms, specifically LinkedIn, should be your best friend as they offer you the chance to enlarge your contacts list at any time unlike events. Exchanging ideas and strategies with diverse people with similar interest is encouraging and influences one's perspective, as well as their motivation to sustain their growth. Also, do not underestimate the importance of surrounding yourself with people who have more experience than you and are willing to show support in your time of struggle. It is crucial to have people to look up to who have already gone through the same difficulties you are experiencing in the present. Not to mention, it's always more productive learning from other's mistakes rather than your own. Remember!

Networking has additional relevant benefits such as providing a space to grow your business' visibility, building confidence or raising your own profile. We all know word-of-the-mouth is an impressive marketing strategy.

Furthermore, motivation is another influencing factor in the process of developing self-resilience and perseverance. Some people find motivation through themselves, while others need outside sources to encourage them to pursue their dreams. However, motivation is the number one factor arousing the decision to advance and grow. I have identified the biggest factor to support my progress in business as seeing the satisfaction in my clients' eyes, as well as, bringing my projects to life and seeing them materialise. In addition to that, the desire to succeed, bring joy and stability in my family's life are also my personal determinants.

Nonetheless, to develop a sustainable business plan, an entrepreneur must launch on a journey of self-discovery, be aware of their capabilities and what skills they lack so they can surround themselves with the right people who can fulfill the gaps. However, growth always comes with new objectives and the only way to discover one's full potential is to begin and pursue. It is essential to face tough situations and experience challenges in order to persevere.

Accepting every failure as a way to develop and learning from them is one of the most important attributes essential to cultivating resilience and perseverance. Additionally, being open to constructive criticism and ideas from the outside not only builds your confidence, it helps you face challenges effortlessly, but also makes you a great leader!

To conclude and going back to my first point in this chapter, success is subjective, only you decide what makes you successful and how you can achieve that. By working hard, being passionate, motivated, and being able to deal with impediments are all crucial characteristics that contribute to balance and support your journey in both business and sustaining your wellbeing.

By Tamika Martin

About The Author

Tamika Martin, from Nottingham, UK is a 3x award winning entrepreneur and businesswoman. Founder of 'Ucreate PR & Events Management Ltd', 'Ucreate Travel', 'Tamika Martin & Friends' and 'Hit Me Up Podcast'. Tamika has successfully launched all 4 businesses from the ground up and is committed, hardworking, and passionate and boasts great leadership skills.

Successful Women In Business – Leadership Edition

She has worked with some high-profile individuals in the entertainment world over the years, appeared on national television frequently and has

Flexed her experience in events at some of the UK's largest events which include: 'The RHS Chelsea Flower Show', 'Royal Ascot', 'BBC Radio 2 Live' and 'BBC Proms'. Tamika is currently focusing her attention on building six figure businesses and creating opportunities for stakeholders. Brand recognition is also one of her key aspirations and goals. Without a doubt, Tamika Martin is destined for global success, she's already on her way!

To Find Out More Visit:

www.tamikamartinandfriends.com

https://instagram.com/tamikamartinofficial

https://linkedIn.com/Tamika Martin

https:/twitter.com/tamikamartin_

Embracing Rosie

Every story starts with a "once upon a time" and finishes with a "happy ever after" and in between the pages there are villains, hero's (in our case heroines), wicked witches, fairies, a few mice and an occasional pumpkin and of course, lost little girls who await the eternal kiss from their Prince Charming.

Rosie Shalhoub's story wasn't always rosy, however it does end in a "happy ever after." She realised the wicked witch was her own critical inner voice, the Fairy Godmother became her "knowing" or as some like to call it her "6th sense" and her Prince Charming came in the form of two very unexpected twins, who were never supposed to have been born and have kept her wide awake ever since. Did we mention her King? He comes later after Rosie saves herself from the damsel in distress she once was, tells the wicked witch where to go and then goes on to save the world.

It was 1967 when Rosie was born, the year dubbed the "Summer of Love" when the Hippie movement was in full swing and the Flower Children were taking over the world. Something must have happened that morning she came into the big wide world, either inhaling too much of the illegal stuff that was floating through the very 60's air or she was reincarnating into a movement of free spirits where she knew she could let her soul run free and wake up 48 years later to find that still the Hippie at heart, this wide eyed girl was about to take the world by storm.

Working in retail ran through her veins as Rosie recalls her very first experiences working in her father's clothing business all but three years old. She would help him put matching shoes back into their boxes, making sure the clothes hangers were all facing the same way and enjoying sitting in the shop window as their very Italian shop merchandiser would turn the windows into something magical. It was no surprise that retail became the very essence of where she built her kingdom and where her love of talking to people started from all those years ago. Where children would be doing whatever children did in the early 70's, Rosie would be down at Shalhoub Bros on Coogee Bay Road talking to strangers and "working" in the family business. A case for child exploitation? Perhaps. However, she grew up learning very valuable skills about business, she learnt how to read different types of personalities and by the time she had grown up she knew how to sell.

After finishing her HSC in 1985 Rosie had no clue what she wanted to do. After taking a course at a secretarial college, which was something you just did back in the 80's, she landed her first real job at AMP. Becoming the personal assistant to the Chief Executive Officer of the department that she can't even remember the name of, Rosie was promoted after only 3 months and was then moved to the stock market department.

She recalls spending time at the stock market, being taking on extravagant lunches, which always turned into dinner, by very wealthy stockbrokers and worked amongst the likes of the then very famous Rene Rivkin, Christopher Skase and Alan Bond.

In 1988 AMP had enrolled Rosie into the Australian Securities Institute where she was trained to be a stockbroker. After achieving high distinctions in all subjects and failing law twice she knew this was not the path her soul yearned for. The fast pace of the city, the long commute and the long hours finally took its toll.

The expensive champagne, the suits and heels and the high salary were swapped for a more laid back lifestyle as she made a complete career move and became an aerobics instructor. Her days were now spent at the gym, her muscles taut and it was here deep in the Sutherland Shire where Cronulla became her home.

In 1993 a freak accident ended her very short lived aerobic career and turned her towards a paint brush. She painted, and she sold. And she sold a lot! Commissions for art work came flooding in.

Rosie fell into a deep depression. Still not knowing what she wanted to do when she grew up. Feeling very unsettled in her then relationship and even more restless within her psyche the needed to find herself and her journey towards enlightenment began. However, somebody forgot to tell Rosie that to become the wise old sage there was going to be a lot of pain, one heck of a journey and a whole heap of synchronicities that the Universe had lined up for her.

Fast forward to 2016 and let Rosie tell you her story for herself... I still remember that day clearly in 1993 as I was vacuuming my hallway and a small voice in my head said "turn the television on". I was born naturally psychic so voices in my head were a part of the norm for me. However I totally ignored it and kept up with my housework when the voice came back this time louder and clearer "turn on the television".

That was weird for me, as I have never been one to watch much television especially during the day and yet the voice persisted "turn the television on.... turn on the television". Doing what any sane person who thought they were going insane would do I turned on the TV.

Falling to my knees in a heap on the floor I wept to the words of Maryanne Williamson as she spoke to Oprah Winfrey in an interview that not only shook me to the core but changed my world for the rest of my life. Sometimes it's those voices in your head, the feelings in your gut the inner knowing from your inside outs that you just can't ignore. There on the screen in front of me were my two idols Oprah Winfrey and Maryanne Williamson who both became the triggers for where I am today.

At that time in my life I was very miserable. Not content in a marriage I was in and totally broke. I spent days in bed with severe depression. Maryanne's words sank through my veins and I knew that I just had to have her book. The voices in my head weren't just in my head after all. Immediately I rang the local book store to hold a copy of Maryanne's book "A Return to Love" where Oprah reviewed the book and in which Maryanne spoke so clearly about "A Course In Miracles".

Successful Women In Business – Leadership Edition

I was told the book was on backorder and I had to wait about a week. I then received a phone call 10 minutes later that a copy of the book was available for $3.00. I was at the store within minutes and spent the next two days with my head in the book, studying every single page and getting lost in every single word. From that moment on I became "me" and I knew that I was on a path to help make this world a better place.

My path was clear now in front of me. I was going to work with what came naturally to me, my psychic ability and my creative art. I had no idea at the time that both my natural talents were going to bring me a life that most girls could only dream of.

Lying in bed a week after my Oprah experience I said a prayer. I asked if I was going to save the world then I needed to be shown how. That night I had a dream where a lady came to me, handed me a paint brush and a whole heap of Christmas balls. From then on "Santa's Little Painter's" was born. That very morning I telephoned Westfield Shopping Centre in Miranda and asked to speak to their casual leasing department and I booked a 6 week stand selling hand painted Christmas balls. Everyone thought I had gone nuts.

With a $5000 loan on my credit card, I had no idea what I was doing but I did it anyway. I had spent the past year or so selling my art from market fairs to market fetes, from trade shows to exhibitions. This was during the time when the Internet was still unheard of so my work could only be shown where ever I could take it. I was exhausted, sick of early morning market stalls that would sometimes make me only a few dollars and where people would hustle till they got things for next to nothing. Winter mornings were literally making me sick and I was over it. I was shown a sign in my dream and like the voice in my head I had to go with it.

Westfield was a far cry from the market stands I was used to. This time around I was playing with the big boys, and play I did. With my credit card maxed out I brought $5,000 worth of Christmas baubles. If I had just a dollar for every person who told me I was doing the wrong thing I could have just made my million then and there. Instead of paying a market stall rent of only $60 a day I signed my life away on a lease of $12,000 for a six week period.

Mind you, I had no money to pay this rent. Instead I did a totally Richard Branson thing and worked out how to do it all after I said "yes" and signed on the dotted line. I felt sick, but I had to believe in my gut feelings, my visions, my inner knowingness. Most of all I had to believe in me.

Looking back now as opposed to where Santa's Little Painter's are today, I would say we did look like a market stall that first year, just a higher end one. I painted my little heart out as queues and queues of people waited in line to get the Christmas bauble personalised. I made my 6 week rent in the very first week I operated. Needless to say, I was officially going to be known as the "lady with balls".

Nobody could remove the smile from my face by the time Christmas day came around. Packing up the site late into Christmas Eve I knew I was onto something after estimating a good little profit for myself that year. Let's just say I made in a 6 week period what most people would make in a whole year, all because I followed a dream, and a literal one at that.

My third year into Santa's Little Painter's became the year I learnt my very first lesson in business in making sure all my t's were crossed and my i's dotted. It was also the year I was taught that not everybody is going to be your friend. My years were filled with clients for psychic readings and they were finished with painting Christmas balls. Life was good, I was making good money and by this stage I had saved enough money to buy myself a gorgeous little bachelorette apartment overlooking the magnificent skyline of the city of Sydney. What was about to unfold however was something that, as a professional psychic, I did not see coming.

I had a wonderful friend who lived in the same apartment block as me. We would spend hours and hours each evening together sometimes over bottles of wine and laugh, and talk and sing and cry. We had a special friendship and I loved her dearly. SLP was in its third year and "A" desperately needed work and money to get her through the Christmas period.

My big heart was excited to have my friend work with me for four weeks and pay her in cash at the end of each day. I was making so much money that I even paid her double what she was entitled to. What harm could that do?

Successful Women In Business – Leadership Edition

Whilst I was helping a friend in need she was counting the dollars in her head.

The week after Christmas had finished "A" asked me if she could go into a business partnership with me. I didn't need a business partner nor did I want one especially one that was such a good friend as I never believed in mixing friends and business. I let her down gently but she was not happy.

I thought it weird that I hadn't heard from her for a week after that very awkward conversation to find a letter addressed to me in the mail from a legal firm. The letter stated that I hadn't paid "A" for a 6 month period she had been working in my establishment (she only worked 4 weeks) and that I had owed her thousands and thousands of dollars. My heart sank, and I thought it was a joke. Knocking on her door I realised when I was asked to leave that this was definitely no joke and I was going to be in big trouble.

Not only did the tax man have his fun with me, the Industrial Relations Court made me feel like the world's biggest criminal. I couldn't understand how this could be as I was the one who was not telling any lies here. I quickly learnt that number one: you don't cheat the tax man and number two: every single business move you make must be put in writing. I fought and fought my case but nothing was going to change as I had done the wrong thing in the first place by paying her cash and not having records to show for it.

The case cost me a lot of money and my solicitor insisted I pay her out on a financial decision as fighting it all the way through the court systems was going to cost me a lot more. Lesson number three: never, ever let your emotions get in the way of making a business and economical decision. I didn't take my own advice though as I wanted to prove I was right. $30,000 later in legal expenses, I don't want to even remember how much was paid out to "A". I was deflated, gutted and totally defeated.

I went away for a long time, a very long time after that experience. I couldn't face the world, it was too harsh a place and the Mediterranean was calling me. Three years later I gave birth to twins, Eliane (pronoucned Elly-Arne) and Joseph. A year after that, I became a single mother, of one year old twins.

Life was presenting itself as a big challenge with two little babies, no financial support and only Christmas to get me through. I was too proud to tell my family and friends of the dire straits I was actually in so there was only one thing I could do.

After I fell to a heap on the floor in my lounge room I got back up like the Phoenix from the ashes and gave SLP all I had. Retail runs through my veins so I knew how to sell, and my art came so naturally and easy to me. I was going to franchise my business. Once again, knowing nothing about franchising I found myself sitting in the office of a well known local accountant who specialised in setting up franchise businesses. Not even baby twins, still in their prams and still breast feeding was going to stop me. I would take the twins to every single meeting I had and if I had to feed them then and there I did. I remember one time at a Westfield meeting I was so unorganised in getting ready to be there on time I threw my jacket on, the babies in the pram and off we walked. I sat down at the meeting to take my jacket off and there in all my glory I had forgotten to put my shirt on! Yes, just me and my very unsexy breast feeding bra in the middle of a busy cafe and very hungry babies.

Back in the accountant's office the accountant thought my idea of franchising was so brilliant that he even had his wife come and sit in on the meetings. We set up the very first SLP franchise in Rhodes shopping centre and here I was starting all over again. Life was good until that following January.

I was asked to have dinner at my accountant's home with him and his wife and I was convinced that we were going to talk about taking over the world with Christmas balls and having Santa's Little Painter's a generic name. History however, was about to repeat itself and instead I was told that the whole franchise business was not a good idea and had no legs to stand on.

You can imagine my surprise when I found out the following Christmas that my franchise idea had been stolen by my accountant. Yes, you read this right. His wife had set herself up in that many shopping centres, there were too many to count. What was the Universe trying to tell me? My ideas, my designs and my whole concept had just been stolen.

Who could I report this to? How could they? Didn't attending meetings with my babies in a pram mean anything to these greedy people? Obviously not. I couldn't report them to anyone, because even though he was an accountant he was also a solicitor and I was very, very, broke, financially and emotionally.

I realised that I must be doing something right if everywhere I turned somebody was trying to take a piece of it from me. They say that the best revenge is success and I used my anger as a fuel, my passion as my motivation and my twins as my driving force. I had lost everything and the apartment that I fought so hard to keep had to go up for sale. My heart was broken and I finally wasn't too proud to ask for help.

You do what you need to do in moments like these even if that meant waitressing. Whilst I waited on tables I had no choice but to turn my lemons into lemonade and I began to actually enjoy the job.

Being the social butterfly that I am I made new friends, became familiar with the regular customers and got to put myself in front of some very high profile people. In case you are wondering where my babies fit into all of this, I have two very amazing parents who stepped in to allow me to do what needed to be done. There are some parts of this story where luck played its role and I am lucky to have the parents I do.

I would have fun with my customers and most of them knew me as the lady with balls or the psychic and some knew me as both. I worked my butt off, I came home to my twins and I planned my following Christmas that I knew was never going to happen as the debt I had accumulated was never going to get me off my feet.

On a chance trip to the bathroom one working day I stopped by to have a chat with my mate Abraham, the owner and brilliant businessman of the Fone King Empire. There were some days I would make myself go the bathroom just so I can have a chat with him and our usual laugh. This day however was different, I was low and sad, I cried in his arms when he asked me how my Christmas planning was going. In all his glory, Abraham became my fairy godfather and before I could blink we became business partners.

Some 13 shopping centres later and Rosie was back! I did what I did best and Abraham did what he did best and together we were a dynamic team. We had a great three years together until once again life was to take both of us in very different directions. Both Abraham and I were presented opportunities that meant we had to kiss each other goodbye and walk down our own yellow brick roads.

I am proud to this day to call Abraham one of my best friends and the most successful and smartest person I have ever met. Whenever I walk past yet another one of his many stores I smile. We finished our last Christmas together with a bang and with Westfield approaching me with an offer I just couldn't refuse. Those days of waitressing paid off, getting to know the managers, staying friendly and grounded and making sure I had my face in front of all the right people. I was offered a shop.

Not only was a shop offered to me, I once again said "yes" without having any idea where the money was going to come from or how as a single mother I was going to pull this off. I signed the lease. I had proven myself with the reputation I had earned with SLP, and I wowed the managers with psychic predictions that always came true. Funny that sometimes my natural talent would at times became my party trick when I needed it to. I knew that life is a game and I had no choice but to play the game well.

The first six months of Embrace's creation we had turned over a whopping 6 figure number. And moving forward six years Embrace has now become the leading provider of spiritual and new age products and the most popular place to go for psychic readings and crystals.

We have had two television shows filmed in our store, celebrities from all over the world come to visit us and we have hosted some of the biggest names in our industry. I am regularly interviewed on radio and I have been interviewed and asked to write an article for the Huffington Post. Before long I had become a public figure and I didn't even know. People come from all over Sydney to visit Embrace as it has now become the hub of the spiritual world. Going back six years upon signing my lease, the accounts manager at Westfield was very much into the whole spiritual/psychic thing and asked me if I would run a festival for Westfield in line with the whole mind, body, spirit theme.

I had no event training and I had no idea of even where to start. This really wasn't part of the plan and I had no intention of running events, however, without wanting to disappoint and really wanting to make an impression with the managers I once again said "yes". That "yes" word was to become my saving grace for with every "yes" I had to learn and grow a new skill. So, in 2010 we put on our first Embrace Spirit and Wellbeing Festival.

Featured on television and with Westfield backing us, the festival went off with a hit three years running. In 2013 however, we hit a huge fork in the road when Westfield went into major renovations and the Embrace festival had to be put on hold. Or did it? A year into meeting the love of my life, Ross insisted I run the festival out of the Sutherland Shire.

God forbid a girl from the Shire actually leaves the Shire. But now he was suggesting I run my business out of the Shire too! So off he dragged me on an excursion day out to look at venues. Luna Park? No! Technology Park? No! The Hordern Pavilion? We opened the door and there in front of my very psychic eyes I saw the whole festival flash before me. "Yes" became that word again and this time I was really out of my depth.

So I had 9 months to put on a festival and this time around I really didn't know what I was doing. I knew if I could create a pigeon pair of twins in a 9 month timeframe then I could do anything. Every cent I had went into the Festival Of Dreams including the children's pocket money and I felt sick. My vision showed me the festival in full swing so I couldn't be wrong but my gut felt sick so maybe I was wrong. The feelings of anxiety out grew me and I got very sick. For the first time in my life I didn't trust myself and I was truly scared.

What made things worse for me in 2014 was that to pull off an event, like we were about to do, was something that huge corporate teams do. Our team was Ross the builder and I, the lady with balls! If ever I was going to need some balls it was going to be now. So, I did what every girl does in times of crisis - I rang my best friend. Harry known as Harry T (the celebrity psychic medium) and I go back a long way and that is another story for another day. Harry my very gay BFF always knew how to cheer me up and cheer me up he did. Sometimes it's not always what you know but who you know. And before my very eyes we had Lisa Williams the world's most famous Psychic Medium with her very own reality TV show signing the dotted line on what was about to become Sydney's most talked about spiritual, health and wellness event.

If I thought I had felt sick before, I felt even sicker now. How was I going to not only run Embrace, be a mum of what is now a family of six children 2 my own and 4 Ross's (now that is definitely another story for another day) and pull off a 2 month period of Christmas balls? Its funny what the human spirit can achieve when your heart and soul is truly in it and when your destiny aligns itself on the right path. I don't think I had ever worked so hard in my whole life. Selling exhibit booths was not as easy as I thought it would be, but now having the divine Ms Lisa Williams name to throw into the selling spiel put us on a whole new level.

People sometimes ask me why I chose the Hordern Pavilion as our venue for the Festival Of Dreams. My answer is always the same, as I wanted an event that was high class, totally and uniquely boutique and somewhere in my thinking I knew that the Hordern would give us instant credibility. It would have been a whole lot easier if we hired a much cheaper venue or even a local RSL venue space but I wasn't going to have it. Embrace is high class and my festival was going to be the same too.

The FOD (Festival Of Dreams) team came together easy once we had signed our contracts - Ross, myself, Adriana and Dianne. (We started with 4 and now there are 8). Days and nights on end we would sit around the kitchen table with children running under our feet, in between soccer and gymnastic training, cooking dinner whilst trying to sound extra professional to potential exhibitors, folding washing as I would dictate emails and running

Successful Women In Business – Leadership Edition

Embrace was truly a year I would never forget. The Festival Of Dreams doors officially opened on 23 August 2014.
Thousands upon thousands of people entered those doors and the media coverage was enormous. Studio10, Sunrise, The Sydney Morning Herald, buses, taxis, posters, we were everywhere! It was almost a bit of a cliché from the movie "Field of Dreams" when the "voice" (the voice I know all so well) would repeat over and over "If you build it they will come". Came they did and Sydney talked.
Our emails were flooded the following week with new potential exhibitors wanting to come on board. We had Hollywood contacting us offering celebrities to attend FOD and I found myself one day totally naked in my shower and laughing out so loud to myself I could have sworn it was all a dream. We didn't call it the Festival Of Dreams for nothing, but the fact that I had finally created my own dream was proving itself a little hard to believe and so I pinched myself to make sure I was still awake.
I was being interviewed on Hollywood radio stations, talking to big US producers over Skype and mixing with movie stars. And so it happened that the 2015 Festival Of Dreams became a Native American theme with Rick Mora and Elder Saginaw Grant. Talk about 6 degrees of separation.
Rick featured in the blockbuster movie Twilight and Saginaw in movies such as the Lone Ranger with Johnny Depp. It was very easy to sell tickets for FOD that year and the once single mother who waited on tables smiled back at me with so much pride that I had to pinch myself again.
Not long after the 2015 FOD I was chatting to a very good friend, well known author and publisher Scott Alexander King from Animal Dreaming Publishing. I have enjoyed reading Scott's work in the past and I like his writing style. Over a very casual conversation one evening I told Scott that I would love to write a book but I have no idea what I would write about.
Scott said that it was easy as you just have to write about something you love. Me being the smarty pants that I always am said "chocolate- I love chocolate, I bet you can't write about that?". Scott proved me very wrong. A year later and "The Chocolate Lover's Message Cards" did not only go to sell

in the European market but an American distributor picked them up and they are now selling across the United States.

All of the sudden I became an International author and I proved Oprah Winfrey right - do something you love and the money will follow. Mind you, my body didn't love me for it but it paid off. We are working on some other big projects at the moment but for now that can wait until after Christmas.

Just in case you're wondering where Embrace fits into all of this since the birth of the Festival Of Dreams, stay tuned to your television screen. "Embracing Rosie" the very first reality show to be based on psychics and spirituality has just had its first season of filming and something tells me that I will be joining my chocolate cards in America very soon in the near future.

The past 12 months has proven itself to be the most exciting in my business career as my overnight success had only taken me 25 years to get here. Santa's Little Painter's is back in the franchise game with every Westfield shopping centre being worked on over the next 5 years. The Festival Of Dreams has become a whole new entity itself taking on its own life that has been filled with magic and awe and even Richard Branson himself has become a fan since his chance meeting with our Native American guests last year.

I believe the secret to my success has been a combination of a lot of things starting with the ultimate belief in myself, in my intuition and in my dreams when everyone else had thought I had gone crazy. If I was to ever give advice to anyone who has had to endure the Tall Poppy Syndrome then I would tell them the same thing I have had to tell myself - concentrate on your own business and never ever be afraid of competition as your competitor will only make you greater than you already are.

I have learnt over the years to ask for help when I needed it and I have even learnt to delegate, which was something I found so difficult to do back in the early days. The busier I am the less work I seem to do these days. Making sure you document everything is advice I would always give and that way there is no room for miscommunication.

Successful Women In Business – Leadership Edition

Always remember your roots and where you came from and always stay humble and grounded. I believe it is important to remember that it is the "little guys" that will make you big and, in the case of retail, it is your regular customers that only need to spend a little with you each week that keep you still standing.

These are the clients that deserve your extra love and care and they surely get it when they walk into Embrace. Remember to always stay in the moment and allow the Universe to conspire to allow all the synchronicities into your life.

I am a firm believer in giving back. FOD works with a charity called Our Big Kitchen in conjunction with Youth of the Streets and Embrace proudly supports the "Free the Bear Foundation". There is nothing more amazing than the feeling of being able to give to another without anything being returned. Financial freedom allows you that and it is in the knowing that another life is being helped because of you.

My career has just been one coincidence after another but it was what I chose to do with those moments that took me from one success to another. Most of all, remember to stay in gratitude, be thankful and grateful for every sale that goes through your cash register. I have not known a sale where I didn't say a silent "thank you", even if it was only for $4.95.

I am grateful when I pay huge tax bills and I say "thank you" because it means that I am making money. I say "thank you" when I pay my staff their wages because without them I wouldn't be where I am today. These are my girls, my "kids" that I like to sometimes call them, my sista's, my friends and my colleagues.

The ones who believe in my dreams as much as I do and I dedicate this chapter to Kati-Rose. Kati was only 14 when she came to work for me, school uniform intact and now 10 years later at 24 I have had the wonder of watching her turn into a beautiful young lady who has become not only my PA, but my babysitter, my nanny and a big sister to my children.

The Festival Of Dreams can be found at www.festivalofdreams.com.au

Embrace can be found at www.embraceaustralia.com.au. Just send us an email, tell me what you thought of my story and how you feel it will help you on your path to success and I will send you an autographed copy of the "Chocolate Lover's Message Cards".

Until next time don't forget to Embrace... Life, Love and Each Other!

Love Rosie xx

By Rosie Shalhoub

About The Author

The girl with a big heart and a massive vision! Rosie, the founder of Embrace, was given a vision at a very young age. She always knew that it was part of her destiny to create an environment of love, peace, harmony and beauty that would be shared by many. Although still stuck in a time warp of the 80's, Rosie has always blamed "it" on the gypsy in her soul. A free spirit with a sense of adventure and an attitude for fun, her style has always been quirky & cheeky mixed in with a whole lot of passion & love.

Rosie comes from a place of authenticity, courage and wisdom. A true believer in the sacred feminine, with the roar of a warrioress, she is a hopeless romantic, living in a world of make believe, fantasy, humour & love.

Embrace is that world. Embrace's success has a lot to do with Rosie's down to earth attitude and easy approach style. Her background in paranormal psychology, her strong 6 sense combined with her passion, grace and psychic awareness gave way to the birth of Embrace. Embrace is a place of beauty and wonder, Spiritual awareness, love and peace. Rosie's main aim was to bring people together through all walks of life as equals. Through humour, joy and laughter she has managed to do this beautifully, creatively and exquisitely.

Rosie is also the founder/CEO of the Festival Of Dreams, a three day event where you can live your dream life. In her words "The Festival of Dreams is a chance to take time out for yourself and embrace new opportunities to be the best person you can possibly be. At the festival you can make yourself a priority in a judgement free zone and work on your own wellbeing, personal understanding and from that, determine to become the best you can be and live your dream life".

Sometimes dubbed as the "lady with balls", Rosie is also the founder of "Santa's Little Painter's" a thriving business specialising in personalised Christmas baubles.

Rosie lives in Sydney with her partner Ross and her twins Joey and Ellie. She is a mother, lover, daughter, sister, friend, entrepreneur, teacher, writer, author, visionary, dreamer and believer.

Successful Women In Business – Leadership Edition

embrace
••• life, love & each other •••

★ Psychic Readings ★

Embracing all cultures, AND faiths

PH. 02 9531 0009
SHOP 1028, WESTFIELD
MIRANDA NSW

Where Real Magic Happens

New Age AND Inspirational Products

WWW.EMBRACE
AUSTRALIA.COM.AU

Find Your Way To Professional Fulfilment With Confidence

Ever since I was a little girl I always wanted to own my business and be my own boss. Doing what? I had no idea, other than I wanted to help people. If I could go back in time and tell that little girl that she'd become her own boss working to help support and guide others as a professional Coach, Trainer, Teacher, and business woman living in Spain; I have a good idea that she would have smiled, said "cool" and carried on playing.

However, this chapter isn't about destiny, fate, things just happening effortlessly or the stars just aligning. This is a story about how even if you don't know what you want, you can still find it. And when you find it, you can learn and become more confident at doing/being it. And you will feel fulfilled.

In this chapter, I will detail my three key learnings in business so far. I will outline the huge benefits to you and your business of; learning how not to be lost, being confident, and feeling fulfilled. I have not only personally experienced the value of these learnings, but I have also supported a large number of Coaching clients such as a successful Advertising executive in their transition to become a Midwife, an unhappy Entrepreneur to leave their first failing business and create two new successful ventures and someone working in an investment bank to become a relationship therapist and business woman. And that is just scratching the surface.

Successful Women In Business – Leadership Edition

I share these learnings as someone who has had the privilege to guide and witness people becoming and accepting a better version of themselves, and go for what they want in life. This is why I do what I do, and why I want to share these learnings with you.

I've been working on my business as well as working on making myself into a business woman for over 5 years now. When I started, I just had an idea. But I had no idea of the time, resources, effort, and heartache that it would involve to make it into a reality. I am proud to be sharing my learnings with you as an entrepreneur who has made many mistakes, one who knows that they will make many more but also as one who is dedicated to taking both herself and those others willing to try, to the next level.

Learning To Not Be Lost

Starting or growing a business is often referred to as a labour of love. I would argue that it is an adventure of exploration. A journey to be found. Working on a business is hard, but it is also confusing and discombobulating. It can force you to put yourself in uncharted waters without a sense of direction. There will be times when you know what to do and where you're going, but there will also be times when you'll feel out of your depth and lost in your entrepreneurial journey.

Being Lost

When you feel unsure of yourself, there can be a feeling of being directionless and stagnant. There's a feeling of discouragement when you don't know where to start, or what to do next to maintain or grow your business and this feeling can stifle your sense of personal and professional growth. There's a frustration and a fog that surrounds when there is this feeling. I know this feeling. When I was in London in 2012 I had this feeling of being completely lost and not knowing where I truly wanted to go or how I would ever get there. Perhaps this resonates with you? If so, please remember that being lost is an inevitable part of a journey, but it is also ultimately your responsibility to find your way and if you're reading this, then I am confident that you certainly are on a journey and it's going to be an adventure filled one. Just like mine.

My journey towards life coaching began in 2012 when I left the metaphorical London fog after questioning my career choice in the charity sector. I knew I wanted more professionally and that I wanted to help people. I left London devastated that the "life map" I had created wasn't leading me to a destination that was fulfilling. In a final attempt to cling to this life map, I decided I needed to confirm if the best way for me to serve people was indeed through charity work. So I left my London life to volunteer with Burmese refugees on the Thai border, 6 hours north of Chiang Mai. With no return ticket. And to make things even more complex and confusing I was also leaving London with a broken heart as the relationship that was also part of my "life map" ended.

At the beginning of volunteering in Thailand, professionally, I was fulfilled to an extent. I was using my skills and experience and helping people. But I was heartbroken after the end of the relationship and I was also mourning the end of who I thought I was in London; someone in a relationship, who knew their passion and had a plan of how to reach their destination. So, even though the London fog had gone, this had simply been replaced by a Thai rainforest mist. Over the next four months I would go for a walk every morning and evening, in the jungle, to the local waterfall or simply along the village road. During these daily walks I started to find peace and answers in the time and space that I was giving myself. And at the end of my 4 month placement I was resolute in two things. Firstly, that it was now or never and I was finally going to live in Spain after wanting to live there for years. And secondly that somehow I was going to help other people to have that time and space for themselves to step back, think, heal, and grow, this was going to be my mission and business. This was going to be my new life map.

Finding myself again was the first step towards the creation of my business. Had I not given myself that time and space, I highly doubt I would have had the perspective to realise that there was another way. And although I had no idea of where I was going. I did have a metaphorical map and a compass. I was no longer lost because I was finding myself. I now know that this is one of the keys to creating and moving forwards in your business. When you take that leap in your entrepreneurial journey, that leap is about you leaving behind who you were and jumping towards who you want to be. Your business is a tool to help guide and support you on this journey of discovery and growth.

Learning Is Finding

Learning about yourself and who you are is key in business. It affects everything from the products/services you provide, to who your ideal clients are, how you want to achieve success, how much success you want to achieve, I could go on. Knowing who you are helps you to work in alignment with your values, your motivation and your goals and vision. When you have a better understanding of who you currently are, you have an anchor, a deeply rooted tree that is better equipped to weather the inevitable storms that you and your business will encounter.

Once it is accepted that learning about yourself is a fundamental part of being a successful business owner and leader, you then need to do it. Now, I am not suggesting that you book yourself a one way ticket to a very remote location for four months. But I do strongly recommend that you start an open dialogue with yourself about who you are and want to be. I recognise that this can be daunting and scary, but so is staying in that frustration and fog. Give yourself the time and space to look up, around and within; and to really start your entrepreneurial journey, even if it may start with baby steps. As Dan Elton famously wrote "The Journey Is The Destination" and when you recognise this and actively start moving on that journey, both you and your business you can never be lost again.

Becoming Confidently Confident

Having worked as a Coach for over five years, I've found that the "journey" looks very different to everyone. I have worked with clients at a wide range of points in their entrepreneurial journey and there has been a common thread in an area that they all needed and wanted to work on: their confidence and self-esteem. They not only want to be confident in what they are doing, but also that what they are doing is enough to take them to their destination.

If you're unsure as to why confidence is so sought after, I invite you to ask yourself two questions. If you were more confident, what impact would that have on you? And what impact would that have on your business?

Self-made billionaire and Spanx Founder and Owner Sara Blakely's advice is "Don't Be Intimidated by What You Don't Know". And this I believe is the root of the issue. When you don't know something, you don't feel confident about it and therefore you don't do it. A lack of confidence becomes an obstacle as it can reduce your willingness to say yes to opportunities or to say no when boundaries are crossed. Risks aren't taken and mediocrity becomes accepted and ultimately expected from both you and your business.

Practice Means Progress

I come from the school of thought that confidence is a skill that we can improve depending on how we interact with it. And when it comes to building up your confidence in business, very few people just wake up and are confident entrepreneurs with all the answers. Consequently, the only way to start to strengthen your metaphorical muscles of confidence is to practice and take active steps forwards, and learn what you (currently) don't know. These steps may be tentative, just as I took when starting my business. They might be firm strides, as many of my clients have taken. Or they might be more leaps than steps, which I took in 2014 when I landed in Madrid, Spain with no flat, no job, no friends and barely able to string a sentence together in Spanish. After having lived in Asia for a large part of my twenties I was confident that I could start a new life. But I lacked confidence in my ability to make a new life on my desired terms, with meaningful relationships and a more fulfilling professional career honouring the promise that I made to myself in Thailand to help give people time and space to think. I had no starting point and no confidence in how I was going to turn my idea into reality, let alone a business.

One way to "not be intimidated by what you don't know" is to take courses and obtain qualifications. And although I am not dismissing the value and importance of training and certifications, it is useful to question if there can be any other action taken, as sometimes there is a point when learning and qualifications can become a form of procrastination. I have noticed, particularly in my female clients, there is a tendency to "wait" until this course has finished or until a qualification has been completed. Their confidence comes in that title or piece of paper. Years ago I read (I can't remember where) that if you want to be a pole vaulter, you can read all of the books, watch all of the videos and speak to all the Pole Vault coaches in the world. But if you really want to become one, you actually have to pick up a pole vault and start to practice being a Pole Vaulter.

In my experience and in the experience of many of my clients, there is so much learning in the doing. So much confidence can be found in taking action. And if this is done in tandem with formal training, well even better. In my case, I was reading books on personal development and Life Coaching, speaking to people working in the industry and watching a lot of TED talks. But it wasn't until I went to see a Life Coach as a client that I was able to see my idea in action. By starting to create the bridge between the idea and the reality, I really learnt and started to gain confidence in my decision. This helped me to take more action, attend a weekend Life Coaching workshop and finally embark on my formal Coaching training. And since then I haven't stopped learning by doing.

How could this technique help you? What things could you do to help build your own bridge between where you are now and where you want you and your business to be? This step may feel intimidating and scary. There will be new bridges to bring your business expansions to the world. But when taking action, remember that it will aid your learning and, at a minimum, improve your confidence in what not to do. There's a line in the song Gone by Madonna that I often say to myself "Nothing Equals Nothing". If no action is taken then no progress can be made. And this I can definitely say, with confidence.

When You Say It, You Believe It. And When You Believe It, So Will Others...

After completing my certificate of training as a Life Coach, I realised that although I could now describe myself as a Coach, I didn't have a Coaching business. I had no confidence in calling myself a Coach and putting myself out there. This feeling was not helped by the "kind words" of a friend's husband when I tried to explain that I was now a professional Coach. He said, "That having a Coach was a waste of time because he had a wife and friends who he could talk to". My confidence in becoming the professional Coach that I now was, continued to take repeated knocks with other people making similar comments. Which, culminated in another friend saying, "Alexa sh*t at life Doman is becoming a Life Coach ha ha ha!" Consequently when people would ask me about my job, I would omit that I was a Coach and just say Teacher. I didn't want to put myself out in the open again, so I shrank.

Whether you are thinking about starting a new business, questioning how and whether you should or thinking about taking your business to the next level, your self-belief and confidence is critical. Have you experienced that? When someone asks you what you do or what you're working on right now, and you play it down? You rush through what it is. You don't hold the space or share the passion you have or the hard work that you've been putting into your business. You are not confident in the journey that you have embarked on. So, apart from taking action, how else can you build your confidence in this area?

I believe that unlike me at the beginning of my business career, you have to go beyond just doing your business. You have to be your business. Every time someone asks you how things are going with you or asks you what you do, this is an opportunity for you to practice being your business. Even if the person is not your ideal customer or a potential buyer, that interaction is a training field for you. A way for you to show up as you now are, the entrepreneur in front of them.

Although I don't necessarily believe that practice makes perfect, I do know that it makes things easier and better. And the more it is worked on, the more confidence one has. When I finally made the conscious decision to start introducing myself as a Coach first, I felt very uncomfortable doing this initially. But the more I did it, the more confident I felt. And as my confidence grew, the actions I was taking to grow my business also grew. I became more present online, started running group workshops, and became more confident in attracting and serving my one on one clients.

As your expertise, knowledge, and businesses grow, you have to continue to create your confidence both consciously and consistently. Ensuring that as you reach new levels of visibility, economic activity and challenge you will be able to draw on the confidence that you already have as well as practice strengthening the confidence you need to have, to reach that next level. And that is when things can really start to take off.

Feeling Fulfilled

Success in business is often thought of in terms of the tangibles; profit, sales, customers/clients, followers on social media and website visitors. As rewarding as it feels to have reached a target or milestone in these areas, I'd like to offer you an alternative perspective, that the ultimate aim for you and your business is that, beyond financial security, it gives you something much more valuable, the feeling of fulfilment.

Fulfilment is that feeling of pride and happiness that your business can provide you with is, in my opinion, one of the most precious and sought after of all the currencies. Feeling fulfilled is the currency that you can cash in and rely on through the challenges and hardships of your business journey. Feeling fulfilled and supported by your business is a source of renewable energy that can help to motivate you to keep going and potentially expand your business in the years to come.

I know from personal and professional experience, my clients and from my market research that for many people, not being fulfilled professionally has a number of negative consequences. And one such consequence is that you feel lost, that something is missing. That "It" isn't enough. Many clients have come to me with what could be argued as "Having Everything". They have the family, the house, the car, the holidays and the lifestyle. But there is something missing. Some of them have tried to fill that perceived void with hobbies, children, a wider social circle; I could continue but you get the idea. And while this may be enough for some, there is a reason why you are reading this book. You want more, professionally. And you've decided that a possible avenue to explore this "More", is your business.

If you're similar to me both now and when I started my business, you want to feel that you're learning. That you're growing. That you're proud of what you do and the product/service you provide. You want to know where you and your business are and where you're going together. You want to go to work with passion and leave with satisfaction. Feeling fulfilled isn't just about taking you and your business to the next level. It's about how you are and how you feel on that journey, that the hard work you will and are putting in will come back to you, not only financially but also emotionally.

Understand Your Why

There are two techniques that I would like to offer that have really helped me in my journey as an entrepreneur. The first one is understanding your why. Why are you starting your business? Why are you sacrificing all of these things? Why do you do what you do? In my case, if I strip down my motivations to their core, I can honestly say that my why is that I want to help people. I want to make people's lives better. That's my why. Of course I can add that I'm extremely interested in why people behave the way they behave. I can even add that I'm curious to see what I'm capable of, not just as a Coach but as a business owner. However, knowing and reminding myself of my why, that helping people is at the core of my business, helps me complete the first fulfilment technique. It helps me to re-frame.

As a solo-preneur or small business owner, you may be all too familiar with administrative tasks that are low in terms of their reward, but high in terms of time required or stress levels produced. What tasks do you dislike? Does appearing on social media fill you with dread? Does negotiating with providers make you feel uncomfortable? Think of these tasks and then connect them with your why. I strongly disliked any form of accounting administration. I would put it off, have it there niggling at the back of my mind. It was a source of discomfort and stress. I'd lose hours doing and thinking about doing these tasks. That is until I re-framed these tasks. I re-framed the tasks and understood that by doing the invoices, spreadsheets and taxes, I was really contributing to the growth of my business, which in turn meant my ability to continue to help people. I re-framed these tasks and this helped me to connect the more tedious tasks with the big picture and the why.

Re-framing helps to put you and not the task back in the driving seat of your business. Many of my entrepreneurial clients tend to be more comfortable focusing on the more junior level activities. They are more used to that. They are confident when dealing with customer complaints, emails and general administrative tasks with a clear start and finish. Thinking strategically is more difficult and more important than day-to-day tasks. However, a CEO's role is to work on the business not in the business. Their role is to sustain current and secure future business. When the dots are connected between the tasks that you dislike but know are essential for your business and the bigger picture. This not only reduces the likelihood of procrastination, but also increases the feeling of fulfilment as the tasks are being done and they are now seen as part of the growth of the business.

Supporting The Building Of Your Business

Has the technique of re-framing resonated and also brought up thoughts of how you can further move from working in the business like an employee, to working on the business like a CEO? If so, this second technique might be of interest to you: the scaffolding plan. Scaffolding is essential to the construction of any building. It's there to support and protect not just the building but the very people building it. Could you build a building ad hoc and without scaffolding? Absolutely. And that's what I did during my first few years in business, but I learnt the hard way that this methodology in the long term will lead to a weak building that could crumble at any time. Planning ahead is your scaffolding. Actively planning for the long term, may feel uncomfortable at first. Remind yourself and practice your confidence in that you have the tools and the ability to learn the future skills needed to become the CEO that you are.

I regularly book in "Board Meetings" with myself where I create, adjust and improve my scaffolding plan. That Board meeting is non-negotiable. It can't be moved from the calendar, just as a real Board meeting would be treated. And during that Board meeting the words strategic and big picture are often used when I feel myself moving towards smaller and more administrative tasks and ideas. This Board meeting is not the time to go through a to-do list, but the time to look six months, one year ahead and set targets and deadlines for projects. It is the place where the outline of your future business is set.

The benefits of scaffolding are enormous. By helping you to think in a strategic way, your focus is on the real build of the business, it helps to keep you on track, to measure your progress, motivate you and reassure you as you have more of an idea where you are going. I know that when I have all of those factors together, I can serve my clients better. I can be a more organised, calmer, more efficient Coach, and this helps me to feel happier and more fulfilled both in myself and my business.

Your Turn

Being an entrepreneur means that you are an adventurer. That you (and I) have a long journey ahead. And perhaps it's already been a long journey, but you know that there is still a long way to go. I have come a very long way from that lost and heartbroken NGO worker living in London. I now find myself in my eighth year in Madrid and my fifth year since completing my Coaching training. My journey (so far) has taken many twists and turns. I've felt frustration at the slow growth, the no growth and overwhelmed with the amount of work. At times I've not known which way to turn or how to get there. But I've kept going and, because of this, I've kept learning and I've kept growing. And I've kept going because I want people like you to succeed. I want you to be who you want and need to be.

You may feel lost during your journey, but when time and space is actively taken to get your bearings and to look at the map and focus on where you are going, you will feel more confident as you move forwards. You will have more motivation to keep going, even when the going gets tough.

And when you recognise that the feeling of fulfilment comes from the journey itself and not the destination, that the confidence comes from the being not the doing and that you can never be truly lost as we recognise that the journey itself is the destination, you can always be found.

Be big, be bold and be brave. Take comfort in the exploration, feel emboldened to step out of your comfort zone and grow your confidence, and continue to seek that self-fulfilment. Your customers, business and CEO (that's you) want and deserve that.

By Alexa Doman

About The Author

Alexa Doman is a British native living in Madrid, Spain. She is a dynamic and energetic International Coach Federation (ICF) ACC accredited Life Coach who works with individuals and teams and puts them in the driving seat to empower them to find their own clarity, take action, and create sustainable change.

Working with others has been part of Alexa's professional journey since she volunteered as an English Teacher in Vietnam at the age of 18. Her volunteer work and English Teaching allowed her to travel extensively in Asia after completing a History and Politics degree at the University of

Birmingham. Her international experience led her to work in the International Charity sector for a number of years in London, before she embarked on her professional Coaching journey.

Alexa currently works as a Coach, Trainer, and Teacher both online and prescencially. She works one on one with her coaching clients, teaches students about personal development, and runs training courses on intrapersonal development. Whomever Alexa works with, she always strives to make real change, empower, and ultimately help those she works with to learn how to help themselves.

To Find Out More Visit:

Website: https://www.alexadoman.com/

Instagram: @alexadomancoaching

LinkedIn: alexadomancoaching

Create the Life You Want

Everyone has a story; everyone's story is interesting. Everyone's life has up and downs, successes and failures, they have felt both love and pain, and they have laughed and cried. I believe I can learn something from everyone's story.

At 49 my life story would take a little more than the chapter I have been allocated in this book, instead I want to share the journey I have been on over the last 4 years. Since 2012, I have been leading a very passionate and profitable life and I love it. That is not to say that I wasn't living a full life before that, but in 2012 something changed. Suddenly, I had put my foot on the accelerator and jumped onto a Formula One track. To understand the last 4 years, you first need to know a little of my history leading up to 2012.

I have always been a driven person, highly competitive and, some might say, a workaholic. I have also been willing to take risks, which is why I left a very rewarding career in marketing to start my journey into recruitment in 1999. At the time, I was the Marketing Manager in one of Australia's largest food marketers and manufacturers. As the Marketing Manager, I was responsible for a team of marketers and managing the recruitment process. The recruitment of staff became the bane of my existence!

What Was So Awful About It?

Firstly, whenever an employee left, it was always poorly timed. They always seemed to resign just when I needed something important done, and inevitably, the rest of the team had to work longer and harder to get it finished.

Secondly, the recruiters I was working with were consistently hard to deal with. They didn't understand me as a client; often, they didn't even bother to meet with me. I felt as though I was wasting time interviewing people who weren't even close to being right and I was getting frustrated.

Successful Women In Business – Leadership Edition

The candidates seemed to be treated like commodities, with the recruiters rarely considering the emotional toll involved with any career move, and that their poor service and mistreatment of candidates reflected poorly on my business.

Finally, these recruiters were too expensive for what they were delivering; A few CVs emailed to me, a few interviews arranged and then a big bill. Where was the expertise? Where was the service? Where was the care? Despite my growing distaste for dealing with recruiters, I had to admit that I needed them. I didn't have the time to sift through hundreds of resumes or the budget to run expensive advertising to find the right candidate.

The realisation of just how bad recruiters were dawned on me in one single, epiphanic moment. I was interviewing for a Brand Manager role within my marketing team. The recruiter, let's call him, "Mr Flick'n'Stick", had sent me the CV of a fantastic candidate. "Super Candidate" had years of great experience but he was a lot more senior than the role required. The recruiter told me, "Super Candidate" was willing to step into a more junior role because he had heard of me and my work, and wanted the opportunity to work with me.

I was pretty impressed with myself. This was my first big Marketing Manager role and hearing that someone had heard of me and was willing to take a step down in order to work in my team was a lovely stroke to my young ego. We've all been there, right? Freshly promoted, intending to build the perfect team and making a name for ourselves. Of course, I was happy to interview this well-credentialed and experienced candidate.

Within the first five minutes of the interview I was burning up with embarrassment. I had started the meeting feeling confident and after a few niceties, I said, 'Thanks for coming "Super Candidate". I hear that you're really interested in joining my team and working with me...' With a blank stare he replied, 'No, not really. I was told that there was a vacant Marketing Manager role. "Mr Flick'n'Stick" said that the business needs an experienced marketer because there is a capability issue.' My heart dropped. This guy was there for my job. He had been told by "Mr Flick'n'Stick" that the marketing team was underperforming. He had no idea who I was or what brands the company owned.

Excuse Me While I Pick Up The Pieces Of My Shattered Ego...

We had both been set up. We call this the 'foil' in marketing. You set up a bad comparison to make your product, service or in this case, candidate, look good. By sending me candidates who didn't fit the brief, "Mr Flick'n'Stick" was making me desperate to fill the role and therefore, more likely to hire someone who was not right but was simply the 'best' of what I had to choose from. Mr Flick'n'Stick was showing "Super Candidate" that he should really consider some of the other roles presented to him, otherwise he may end up working in a lower level job for a new manager like me.

I couldn't believe this recruiter's lack of processes and ethics. There was no partnership or expertise sharing and I was angry at the time wasted and the disrespect shown to both the candidate and me. This experience had well and truly burst my bubble and planted the seeds for my first business.

About 18 months after this incident I resigned from my job. With no idea about running a small business, let alone a recruitment business, I started Market Partners with my good friend, Sacha Leagh-Murray.

The vision behind Market Partners was simple: If sales and marketing professionals recruited for sales and marketing roles, life would be easier. I wanted to create a recruitment agency that I would want to work with. I wanted to be a partner and an advocate, and to share in the risk and reward. Ultimately, I wanted to work with people and companies that I liked and respected and to help them grow to have the businesses, teams and careers that they wanted.

Over the next twelve years, we grew the business and in 2008 we merged the business to become a national entity called Carrera Partners. The following 4 years saw us build a good reputation in the market place with offices in Melbourne, Sydney and Brisbane. However, things just weren't right. As a leadership group, we wanted different things and wanted to take the business in different directions. Our purpose, passion and values were no longer aligned. I was finding it difficult to stay engaged and I no longer felt I was adding value. I didn't love my work anymore.

In November 2012, everything changed. I was given an amazing opportunity to travel to Uganda with not-for-profit, The Hunger Project, and I haven't looked back since. Up until this time in Uganda, I had always thought that I was a global citizen. I am educated, aware, caring and I thought I understood the complexities of issues such as hunger, poverty and injustice. I thought that I knew about the plight of the worlds poorest and that I was contributing to a solution, after all, I sponsored two World Vision Kids, bought presents from Oxfam and gave donations to every charity event my friends and family participated in. However, it was not until this trip that I was confronted with what it was really like to have limited or no opportunities or choices. It opened my eyes and I saw the real impact of hunger, poverty and injustice.

Many of the things I saw, experienced and felt in Uganda are difficult to describe. What I did learn is that I had no right to complain about my life. I had no right to waste the opportunity I had to live the life I wanted. I am blessed to have been born into a life where I take the basics of food, warmth, education, healthcare, safety and even love, not just for granted, but as an entitlement. This is not the case for many around the world. I had been accepting all of this as a given, in the same way I was accepting that I had to stay in the business and job because it was 'the safe option'. Going to Uganda gave me the opportunity to question everything and to discover and appreciate that I had choices.

When I returned from Uganda, I had changed. It felt like I left Uganda with the heart, courage and determination of the women I had met there. These women were brave, they were resilient, they never complained. Why bother complaining when no-one was listening? They were purposeful and grateful for everything they had, they didn't wallow in thoughts about what they didn't have. So, I came back and viewed my life through a new lens. Instead of fearing risk and change because of what I might lose if I failed, I looked at my life through the lens of what I already had and how grateful I should be for it all. The thought of failure no longer scared me, instead I saw it as a blessing that I could make new choices, take different directions and to strive for more. Perhaps my most significant realisation was that life is very precious.

If I had been born in Uganda instead of Australia, there is no doubt that I would be dead. I had my second child at 40 years of age and there were complications. I barely survived the complications with the best medical attention money could buy, let alone if I was in Uganda or another of the world's poorest countries. I came back realising that every day is precious and needs to be lived. For so long I had been living for the future, "when I pay off the house I can do what I love", "when I get the kids through school, I can travel more", "when I get my superannuation to a point that I can retire comfortably, then I can think about helping others". I realised, I could be dead before I achieve any of those things so I needed to start living now.

I had changed and consequently, I changed everything. My business, my business partners, where I was going to send the kids to school and where we were living all changed. Though, I did keep my husband. It was after this life-altering experience that my life seemed to move into warp speed.

In January 2013, a few months after my return, we sat down as a family to discuss our commitment to The Hunger Project. The Hunger Project works on a Global Investor model. As a Global Investor you commit to a minimum donation or investment of $5,000 per year. With my 4 and 7-year-old sons and my husband we worked out what we had to change to find that $5,000. In the end it really wasn't that hard. We ate in a few extra nights a week, we had a few extra alcohol free days, my husband and I took lunch to work a few days a week and the kids agreed to one less present from us at Christmas and to help around the house for no pocket money. We have since found that our commitment to find $5,000 not only helps many around the wold but it has been of great benefit to our health and our family.

Shortly after my trip I was asked to join the Victorian Development Board the Hunger Project and within 12 months I was appointed Chair. When I was first approached about joining the board, of course I was flattered and excited, but I was also nervous. How was I going to fit it all in? I was running a business and raising a family, I was already so busy, how much more did I have left to give?

The funny thing is when you are passionate about something, it doesn't feel hard or like work and somehow you find the time. It just happens. Every time I attend a board meeting, or I meet someone who is inspired by the work we do at The Hunger Project and wants to help, I feel even more blessed, more energetic and more empowered to be better and do better. There is something incredibly uplifting and soul nourishing to do something for someone else, for the good of others, without any expectation of something in return.

On returning to Melbourne and my business, I realised I couldn't work the way I had been working. I was miserable and the business wasn't doing well. Not only was it soul destroying, there wasn't any financial reward. There was no reason to stay except for the fear of the unknown. Since 2012, I have been busy creating the life that I want. It has taken a lot of work, some risk and a few ups and downs but it has all been worth it. Let me tell you what I have done.

I Got My Business Right

Just over six months after returning from Uganda, with the support of my amazing husband, my family and one of the business partners we demerged and started again. In a period of 5 weeks we rebranded ourselves and In June 2013, Chorus Executive was born.

After years of poor performance in its' previous form, since 2013 Chorus has had double digit growth, year on year, for the last 3 years. Our success has allowed us to launch 2 new service lines – coaching and personal branding and double the size of the team. We have won a number of awards including Top 5 Most Socially Engaged Recruitment Agencies in Australia and I was named a finalist in the 2015 Telstra Business Women's Awards.

I Invested In Learning

The world is changing fast and to stay relevant we have to change with it. I mentioned previously that Chorus Executive launched 2 new services – coaching and personal branding in 2013. Although, as an executive recruiter and head hunter, I have been offering career coaching for over 15 years, I had never completed an actual qualification. My philosophy has always been if you are going to do something, do it right, so in November 2013 I enrolled myself in a Post Graduate Diploma in Organisational Change and Executive Coaching. This 12-month course took me over 2 years to complete but I did it. I wanted to make sure that I could offer my clients the very best of me and now I am confident that I can.

I Spent Time With The People Who Are Most Important To Me

In March of 2014 our entire family, including my mother, went to Las Vegas for our 10-year wedding anniversary. I wore my original wedding dress and we renewed our wedding vows with Elvis. We spent 5 weeks travelling around the US. We went to Disneyland and drove a campervan around the Grand Canyon, San Diego, San Francisco and LA. We did everything we wanted to do and it was amazing.

In the planning stages for this trip we had many people discouraging us with so many reasons why we shouldn't; "The exchange rate is too high", "It isn't the right time for business". "Wait until the kids are older", etc. etc. etc. I refused to continue only living my life for the future. We needed to live now.

Of course we have to be sensible, but we also have to enjoy the present. 3 years on and my boys still talk about our incredible trip, the time they got to spend with us, but most importantly the time they spent with my mother – their grandmother. On our return my mother said, that the 5 weeks she spent with us travelling were amongst the best days of her life. Now, isn't that worth it?

I Started To Say, "Yes", Instead Of Finding Reasons To Say, "No".

We are presented with so many opportunities every day and yet I feel we are hardwired to say no without really understanding the reasons why. I started making a conscious effort to do this. I started saying, "yes", instead of finding reasons to say no.

This new approach had me saying, "Yes", on a whim, to another 3 trips, all of which were to prove just as life-changing as my Uganda trip. In January 2015 I went to Antarctica. 6 months later, I was on Necker Island with Richard Branson and in January 2016 I went to the Amazon.

Of course I "shouldn't" have taken these trips. Everyone had an opinion – the cost, the time away from the business, my time away, from the family, what will your husband say? Thankfully I didn't listen because these trips have created opportunities I'd never have had, if I didn't say yes.

I have made lifelong friends and business associates from these trips, including one new business partner. I have found mentors who have helped me to grow my business and I was inspired with a new business idea. And, I drank Veuve in the pool with Richard Branson on Necker Island!

I Wrote A Book – We All Have A Book In Us

As I said at the beginning of this chapter, I think everyone has an interesting and inspiring story. Most people are too scared to share it, not me. In February 2016, whilst in The Amazon, I launched my first book Hire Love – How to Hire Passionate People to Make Greater Profit. This book shares my story but also shares the Chorus Executive methodology of recruitment. Our fundamental belief is that people deserve to love their work and employers need their employees to love what they do if they are to achieve the business results they desire. During this process I was questioned as to why we would want to share our methodology and give away our secrets for success. My answer was simple. Organisations may not have access to our service or may not have the resources to work with us but they still need to hire the best people for their organisations. That's our vison at Chorus Executive, for everyone to love what they do as much as we do and to empower possibilities by creating powerful and profitable connections.

I Took Another Big Business Risk

During one of my trips it dawned on me that the recruitment industry really hasn't changed in many years. Job boards such as seek.com.au in Australia and LinkedIn have created a more transparent and direct market place between job seekers and employers but the actual process has not changed much. This trip allowed me to get away from the day to day, I was able to be inspired by those around me as well as by my surroundings and I came up with the idea of creating an online version of what we do.

In 2016 we launched Peeplmatch.com, an on-demand candidate curation service where job seeker and employer matching is based on more than just skills and previous experience. This will be a revolution in recruitment.

We know, and there are thousands of research studies supporting this, that to be good at a job is more than just having the skills to do the job. You need to respect your manger and team, you have to feel aligned to the values and culture of the organisation, you need to believe that what you and what the business is doing, is important. Of course you also need to feel valued and rewarded and that you are adding value and making a difference with what you do. Current recruitment technology does not allow for this. Existing technology helps jobseekers and employers connect quickly or cheaply, but will not necessarily help you find the job that you, as a talented person, will love. That is the Peeplmatch vision – to work with job seekers to find jobs they will love, in organisations where they belong. We have only just launched so watch this space, there is more to come.

In 2012 I was running a business and a family, I thought I was busy and didn't have time. Clearly I was wrong. Look what can be done with a bit of prioritising and a belief that anything is possible. Look what you can achieve when you have a clear vision of the life you want.

It has taken me a long time to get me to this place. Like many people I just kept doing the same thing because it is what I thought I had to do, what I was meant to do. I had to get to the point where I was crying everyday as I arrived at work before I realised that it just wasn't worth it.

To create the life and career I have now, I had to pull everything apart about my old life, in particular, all my misconceptions about what I "should" or "could" do. I had to stop listening to others, who always had an opinion about what I should do, and start listening to myself. This does not mean that I don't ask for or take other people's advice; it just means that I no longer place more value on the opinions of others than on my own.

Here Are My 10 Tips For Creating The Life You Want:

1. Take Time Out -for you to understand and reconnect with yourself. This might be little breaks, or like me, it might be a life changing event like going to Uganda with The Hunger Project. Not only do we need the time but we deserve it. If people call you selfish for taking this time, smile graciously and ignore the comments. Once, when talking about my travels I was once told that I had a "long leash." I ignored the comment but when I told my husband he was really offended. "You are not a dog," was his response.
2. Understand What Providing For Your Family Means - it is more than a house and paying the school fees. I find too many people live with a sense of duty and obligation not passion. I want my children to live passionate and happy lives, not lives of material comfort at the expense of self-actualisation and happiness. In 2013 when I decided to de-merge my business and start again, with all the financial and emotional risk this entailed, we spoke about this as a family. My husband's stance was, "If we have to sell the house, we will sell it. As long as you are happy and the kids are healthy, we will be fine." The children's response was, "Just be happy mummy, so you can play games with us again!" I will always prioritise the happiness of my family and myself over a new car or an overseas holiday.
3. Practise Appreciation - take time to appreciate all that you have to be grateful for. Funnily, we usually compare ourselves to those we think are "better" than us – better job, bigger house, smarter kids. If you consciously stop yourself doing this and start to see the world through a different lens, you will see that in fact, you are blessed already. Trust me, when I tell you there are more people who have less than you – less money, less health, less love and worse jobs than you.

Successful Women In Business – Leadership Edition

4. Believe That You Have Choices - it is really easy to feel stuck and that you "have no choice". At the end of my time at Carrera Partners I felt stuck. I had to go away and take time out of the business to realise that the constraints, "being stuck", was only in my mind. We always have choices. We just have to be open to see them and then be brave enough to make a choice.

5. Surround Yourself With Amazing People - and weed out the rest. Just because you have been friends with someone since high school doesn't mean that they have to be in your life forever. If you walk away from someone feeling less energised or drained get them out of your life. I am not saying that you can only have happy friends. What I am saying is that those around you should support you, inspire you, challenge you and make you feel good when you are not feeling it and care. That is also your role as a friend. If you find that your relationship is one sided get out of it. It can be hard, but trust me when I say you will feel so much happier when you have the right people around you.

6. Be Smart With Your Resources - when you have resources you have choices. Your resources include:

a. Money - Don't spend more than you earn, it's as simple as that. If you are smart with your money this gives you the opportunity to take your dream job even if it is paying less than your current role, to start a business, go back to study or do anything else you are passionate about.

b. Time – Learn how to say no. Spend time with people you love and admire, doing things where you can learn and grow. The concept of FOMO (Fear of Missing Out) is outdated.

c. Energy – Focus your attention and energy towards positive outcomes not negative thoughts. Dwelling on the negative and stewing over what is wrong just drains you more.

People – Use the strengths of the people around you. Ask them for help. Too many of us, believe that asking for help is a sign of weakness, a sign of failure. I think it is a sign of strength. Why struggle along alone, when you can ask those around you for help and create a better result.

7. Be Brave - Stop using the words should, shouldn't and can't. Dare to dream and allow yourself to fail. Be open enough and brave enough to deconstruct your life, analyse it and recreate it. Sometimes you have to break it first before you can recreate it. Whenever I get scared about a decision I am reminded of something I read once; when a toddler learns to walk they fall over again and again and again. They have no concept that falling is actually failure or that they are "bad", "useless" or "unsuccessful". They just keep getting up until one day they walk. This is how I like to live my life. I have fallen down many times, but I have also run marathons! (Metaphorically speaking of course.)

8. Give Without Expectation - it is amazing how good you feel when you actually give without expecting anything in return. Giving your time, money or even a compliment can have such a positive effect on the recipient. I find it is incredibly humbling to give with no expectations, just to be of help and assistance to some-one else and adding to someone's life, it helps keep me grounded. Expecting nothing back makes whatever you give a true gift, rather than an impersonal transaction.

9. Learn To Celebrate Yourself - guess what? You are not perfect. And you know what? You don't have to be. Learn to accept yourself and love yourself. As I have got older it has been easier to do this. I now know what I am good at and probably more importantly, what I am not good at and I have finally accepted that I am not great at everything and never will be. Don't beat yourself up for all your failures and weaknesses instead; celebrate your strengths and successes.

10. Believe That It Will Be OK In The End - some may call this optimism: I just think I am being practical. In the words of Oscar Wilde, "Everything is going to be fine in the end". If it's not fine, it's not the end."

Thank you for taking the time to read this chapter. I hope you got at least one insight from these words that could be beneficial to your life. If you have any questions or comments, please feel free to contact me on chris@chorus-executive.com.au

By Christine Khor

About The Author

Christine Khor - founder of Chorus Executives. It's taken fifteen years of risk-taking, innovation, dizzying wins and dismal losses to make Christine Khor the successful business owner she is today. After a long and successful career working in product and marketing management for leading companies such as Kraft Foods and Simplot, she started her own specialist recruitment consultancy in 2000 with the very simple premise; that sales, marketing and communications people should recruit for sales, marketing and communication jobs.

Her business has undergone three major transformations to get to where it is today. The first was the birth of Market Partners, which survived a brief encounter with an embezzler, cornered the Melbourne market for sales and marketing professionals, grew in size and reputation and then considered expanding nationally. The expansion resulted in a merger with a Sydney based business and thus Carrera Partners was born. With offices in Melbourne, Sydney and Brisbane, the business was now nationally recognised, however after nearly five years, the relationships of the four directors became strained with differing visions for the future of the business. It provoked Christine to run away to Africa in order to gain perspective and bring meaning back into her life. She volunteered for The Hunger Project – a not for profit organisation that works to eradicate world hunger, and came back from Uganda a changed woman.

Her adventure lent her the strength to make the bold decision to demerge from Carrera Partners in 2012 – it was to be her biggest challenge yet, but resulted in the best payoff; the birth of Chorus Executive. A business that is wholeheartedly built on her values and vision; Chorus Executive is a holistic talent management company, providing recruitment, coaching and personal branding services to the sales, marketing and communications space. Her Melbourne staff remained with her and supported her through the transition.

A self-proclaimed change-junky, Christine lives for innovation and growth. She is a passionate speaker on career building, leadership, gender equality, work/life balance, small business start-ups and fulfilling your dreams.

At Chorus Executive, Christine specialises in coaching, mentoring, executive recruitment and organ-isation development.

She is also the Chair of the Victorian Development Board of The Hunger Project. Christine recently adventured to Antarctica as part of The Unstoppables, travelled to Necker Island to join Richard Branson and a number of other prominent business leaders to discuss leadership, business and innovation, and was named a finalist in the Telstra Women's Business Awards for 2015.

Christine has also recently published her first book, Hire Love, to share her insight and knowledge on how to recruit passionate people to make greater profit and is the founder of Peeplmatch.com.

Successful Women In Business – Leadership Edition

Defining Success

To be a successful woman in business means many different things to each woman. Whether your take is financial success, or success based on your reputation or whatever you choose it to mean for you.
I choose to believe that being a successful woman in business means to be a business that contributes to others, that is game changing in an industry that comes from a place of heart and purpose. While allowing me to do what I am meant to do, to unleash my own inner brilliance and genius and do what I am passionate about. That then supports my life, my lifestyle and allows me to continue to be the best mum possible for my two children who are nearly 9 and 7 ½ years of age. That is the big version of being a successful woman in business.
Or I could say 'being a successful woman in business allows me to do what I want, when I want and how I want and that is for the benefit of me and others'.
Being in business for me prior to my life reboot of 2012, I had been in the travel industry for 15 years. A job I loved and worked very hard at and a job that had a lot of stress to it also. I ran this business from home once I fell pregnant in 2007 and it enabled me to have an amazing lifestyle working from home. It allowed me to fully love and enjoy both my pregnancies and be able to relax with the changes more so than if I had to rush into work and was concerned about being late.
I loved working from home and being my own boss and being able to network and attend events when I wanted to. I was able to work when the babies were asleep and work fitted into my routine and the kid's schedules. Running my business from home also meant that when my marriage ended and I was finding it hard to focus, that I could take the time off I needed. I could step away from the desk and get fresh air when I needed.
Then being a single mum and running my own business from home felt rather daunting and scary but then empowering at the same time. For the last 4 years I have been able to do this. I have been able to be at the school when I needed to be and when my kid's E & K asked me to be present. So this for me, felt like success.

But something inside me wanted more. I knew that I wanted to be more than a 50 year old travel agent. There was a drive and a yearning inside my heart that wanted more. While I knew I could be happy going with the flow and continuing running the travel business from home, I had heaps of friends who were still loving and thriving. I just knew I wanted more but I had no idea what that was going to be or how I would do it. I simply did not know what I did not know.

Then I guess, sometimes like having the shakes, you awake and say: 'here is your wake-up call. You wanted more, here is the more you asked for.' It might not have exactly been how I wanted it, but I know that sometimes we don't get what we think we want, we get what we need. But we do get what we ask for….

My reboot and my 'more' took the shape of my marriage ending at a time in my life that I consider to be my version of rock bottom. I felt completely shattered and broken at the time. I felt alone, insignificant, confused, scared, worried, afraid, sad and was suffering high anxiety at the time. I did not recognise the woman I saw in the mirror. I did not like the way I was feeling. I was concerned about my future and the kid's future. How would I cope and survive? What had I done to deserve this? Why couldn't we make our marriage work for the sake of our family?

These are normal questions that go through your head at the time, but extremely un-empowering at the same time. Normal and ok. What would I do next?

Run off (well fly off) to the McLaren Vale and drink Shiraz for 4 days is what I did, while being supported by my dad and his wonderful wife, as this was where they lived - and what a place to 'drown my sorrows' so to speak. The kids stayed home with their dad while I had some much needed time out for me. It was here, in South Australia's finest wine country that I started to heal. I started my journey of searching for information that would help me figure out my next steps. It was wise words from Bev, my dad's wife, 'I think you need to accept your marriage is over and make new plans when you go home'.

So I did. I fumbled my way through most of it though. The Googling and talking to people, friends and others. Here were some clear steps forward, a check list of sorts that would show me what to do. It was much easier to get married, so why was it so hard to get un-married? Was I separating or was I getting a divorce, how does this all work and where is the right information? Surely it can't be that hard and do I really need to run off to a lawyer right now?

I had no idea what to do and actually, I did not want to do anything right now, I just wanted to be able to 'be' and sit with the feelings and emotions. Then I would get around to my next step forward. I went through the motions and focused on my own inner health so that I could be the best mum at the time for E & K. I did get some legal advice and then some more and then I was served papers for court. Talk about being rocked at your core and kicking you while you are down. That is how I felt at the time.

Then jump 12 months ahead, working away in the travel business and I have just come back from Las Vegas on my divorce holiday. All in the name of research. The travel business was focusing on health retreats and now I had an idea for divorce holidays. I was chatting to some industry colleagues not long after I had come back from a stunning health retreat in Thailand. I was getting comments on how great I looked and asked what I had done to heal. I knew that I needed to go on another solo holiday and go somewhere warm, where I could get pool side service, room service, where there was action and adventurous activities. I wanted to shop and go to day spas and then dance the night away. Where else in the world could I do this? Las Vegas of course. Being completely honest, I also wanted some attention and to get my flirt on. I was ready for that.

I was completely focused on the divorce holiday idea but also because I was being asked so often how I got over my divorce so well. I then wanted to help other women going through a separation and divorce too. But I wasn't a counsellor a psychologist or a coach. I was just little ole me, the girl next door. The girl next door still had that inkling inside that she wanted more. Again, I did not want to be a travel agent in 20 years' time, I had just turned 40 and still wanted more. Then while working away on the divorce holiday idea a business coach said to me, 'Renee, whenever you talk about helping others through their divorce, you light up, your voice changes.' Yes, I said. 'So, just go do that, be the Divorce Go To Girl'.

It was like someone had given me permission to go after what my heart was telling me to do, I just had to get my 'head' out of the way. Take all the logic aside and just follow my intuition and this yearning inside. It was like someone had turned a light on inside me. I have never looked back, only forward to all the possibilities.

Finding Purpose & Passion
However, it was not until I attended a workshop run by Carolyn Tate on "Purpose" that I realised I could actually change my career and start a business because I had found my purpose and my passion. I used to think 'doing what you love' is for sports' elite athletes or rock stars. I didn't think the 'girl next door' could do that. Wasn't I just supposed to 'get a job' and do that? Keep on keeping on with being a travel agent? Now, don't get me wrong I have loved the industry and understand it is a more challenging job than many people understand. I just wanted more.

I knew in my heart of hearts and felt with every bone in my body that helping others through their separation and divorce is what I wanted to do and just had to do. Trust me, working in this space, I have thought about quitting it many times. Hearing about all the hurt people do to each other at the end of the marriage, and during also, does make you want to cry. Then I think, how would I be fulfilled doing something else? Would 'x' job fill my cup up? Would I be making a bigger difference in the world? The answer is always no. I know that I must show people how to see the flip side to their separation and divorce.

When you work with people going through one of life's most challenging times, and the feedback is 'you are my earth angel' or even one lady was considering committing suicide one night when I spoke to her for a few hours. She is alive and well and seeking further help now. When you are up doing coaching until 1am because someone needs you that much (extremely rare) you know you are on purpose with what you are meant to do. This to me is success: doing what you are passionate about and that has a purpose. Seeing people come through their separation and divorce a renewed version of who they are, and thought they were, is extremely fulfilling. To help others shortcut their time frame in how they feel about getting back into life is very rewarding. When women (and some men) learn how to see the opportunity in their new start is what lights me up. As they understand the roles they played in the relationship and how they got to where they are now, brings my clients to the place of acceptance, which is the first phase in true healing and moving forward.

People come to me in person or on line or on the phone and they are in a world of confusion, just like I was, and they have no idea where to even start with the whole process. Which is why I created my free online Beyond The

Breakup Boot camps. To deliver a week's worth of information to help with their steps forward and then the emotions behind their feelings is how I contribute and give back to people in the early days of separation.

My Mission And My Why

Now jump 4 years on from my marriage ending and I feel like I have gone through my own 'tsunami of a divorce' and I can see a big gap in the market for helping couples separate successfully together, and stay out of court. From working with lawyers, mediators and the court system, I have experienced a lot.

My big mission now is to change the way 'we' as a country and society actually do separations and divorce. Mostly all of our actions and emotions come from a place of fear and other negative emotions like anger and resentment. No one really wants to talk about divorce, but I know we need to. We need to talk about it so we know we can do it better and differently. To divorce from a place of kindness, and exit the marriage or untie the knot just like we came into the marriage. Being civil and kind. I know, mixing those words into the divorce space doesn't really seem to match. That is a good thing.

We need to be authentically amicable and be focused on the best interests of our children. There needs to be a bridge to fill the gap between couples and their lawyers and help them deal with the emotional roller-coaster that lies ahead. Plus, what the right steps forward are. By educating, inspiring and empowering the individual and the couple to see their separation and divorce as an opportunity for a new beginning. To divorce with kindness, compassion and empathy.

The way we have been separating and divorcing is not helping those actually going through the process. Divorce costs the Australian Government 14 billion dollars a year.

http://www.news.com.au/lifestyle/relationships/marriage/divorce-is-costing-the-australian-economy-14-billion-a-year/news-story/e5a101ea76351d4ba145279011b934ac

However, the emotional costs outweigh the financial. We can make more money, but we can never get back time. Depression is also a common occurrence after a marriage ends and you are likely to go through very similar stages of grief as if someone had died. Sometimes this is even harder to deal with as this person is still in your life. So we need to encourage healthy relationships post separation. Women and men move on differently from each other because we are wired differently as humans. I do feel that we need to come together during this time and work out the separation together. No taking sides and fighting each other. We just have to have awareness and separate differently. For the sake of our children but also ourselves, our own healing and journey so we are the best parents for our children and our children's children.

What if we could end our marriage in a more 'aware' state and have the conversations we need to have with our partners, the way they need to had? Not with fighting through lawyers and the court system. What if we could take the emotions out, just for a bit, and focus on the future. Not what he did or she did and understand there are three sides to every story, his side, her side and the truth. That no one is really at fault or to blame. We all participated in the relationship.

The truth is we aren't taught how to have successful and lasting relationships. We definitely are not taught now to end them consciously either. As divorce rates rise to nearly 50% and then second marriages are around 75% divorce rate, wouldn't it be great if we did relationships differently and also spent time healing before we moved on?

My why continues on to be about my E & K, my wonderful kids and the legacy I am going to leave them? Before all that though, I need to be my best to be their best. I know many women after they have children, then put their children first. Which seems normal and the status quo. However, when we don't put ourselves first we then forget about our own needs and how we need to be filled up with love to be able to give our over flow to our children and partners. Without putting ourselves first, then a little bit of resentment builds and builds and bubbles over. We then start to feel unappreciated. None of this helps anyone. We need to know our worth and that generally it is the woman and mother keeping the family unit together by taking care of the family. Sounds old school but it is generally how a family functions. Which is why we need to be full of love, to take care of ourselves and then others.

With putting ourselves first, then comes finding the harmony between it all, or maybe that is balance for some, or just being flexible. Have a life which is in harmony and balance is when we are in flow and everything is all working as we would like. Which is why I find working for myself and doing what I want and when I want enables harmony and balance.

It's knowing how to take care of that little rollercoaster rides of life that may happen along the way.

That is what matters most, and again, when our love tank is full and we are taking care of ourselves first, we are able to deal with the ups and downs and sideways and this ways and that.

Taking care of our business, on all levels, whether they be spiritual, personal, professional, social and any other area you need to take care of, by filling all those areas of our life, is another version of success for me. Do these happen all at the same time? Mostly, but occasionally they are off balance, but that is ok, that is life. It is how we bounce back and fill up our own personal tanks that matters.

For me, this is what being a successful business woman is all about; doing what I am meant to do and serving others from a place of love. A big mission, absolutely, will I need help sharing my message? Every day, all day.

By Renee Catt

About The Author

After going through her own 'tsunami' of a divorce, Renee became known as the Divorce Go To Girl and is sought after for her expert advice on separation, divorce, and beginning again as a single mum. She was also labelled as a 'Divorce Guru' by Kiis FM and has been seen across many media publications. Renee saw a gap in the market to help couples separate together, with kindness and now helps to bridge the gap between the unknown of separation, divorce and seeing a lawyer. Her company is called Separation Success. She aims to change the way people view their divorce and how they separate and move forward. Bringing in her own strategies, other experts and being a qualified coach and mentor, Renee helps couples move through the emotional stages of their relationship ending as they know it, encouraging couples to maintain an authentically amicable relationship in the future.

If You Would Like To Find Out More, Visit Renee's Website At:

www.separationsuccess.com

Successful Women In Business – Leadership Edition

Curating Your Success

I remembered it vividly.

The Secretary-General of the United Nations Ban Kim-moon was speaking to an audience primarily made up of young business men and women. I counted. I was 8 seats away from where he was standing. It was only a day earlier that I stood in the exactly same spot where the Secretary-General was standing as I facilitated a Summit session on the theme of young people and world peace.

I was at the United Nations Headquarters in New York City. Needless to say, my 2-day visit to the iconic place in July 2016 was a highlight for me both personally and professionally.

At 37 years old, I am a global business consultant, an award-winning graphic designer, a business writer, an international speaker and trainer and an avid traveller who happens to hold a long list of qualifications of which includes a doctoral degree.

I cannot say I planned to walk the career path that I am on right now as a lot of my accomplishments came as unexpected, but my accomplishments are not completely accidental. I attribute my success to a combination of having an innovative mind-set and a series of strategic manoeuvres, a powerful combination that has served me well.

Specifically, there are 5 strategic manoeuvres that I have benefitted from greatly throughout my career.

Manoeuvre 1: Don't Fall Into The Trap Of Indecisiveness By Asking Yourself The "10 Years' Time" Question.

People always find it interesting, some even gasps in surprise, when they find out my background. As a former medical scientist, I hold a doctoral degree and specialised in vascular medicine or study of blood vessels. People find it fascinating that I would abandon a hard-earned medical research career to embark on something totally different. At times I too find it hard to explain. I do, however, remember the feeling that I had towards the end of my clinical research career. After years of working in hospital, I had nailed my routine and perfected the research procedures and techniques to a point that, if I was allowed, I could probably conduct my research with my eyes shut. As my work became a routine so was my restlessness.

I knew I had to make a change and that change was difficult. To start with, I worked very hard to become a doctor so I could contribute to scientific discovery; it was a noble career. I also had cultural pressure. As a young female Asian research doctor, I was seen by many as the one that others would inspire to. I had the brain and I had a respectable and intellectual job; it was almost a crime to give it all up to do something completely different. Of course, I knew I was not the first or only person to decide to change gear and start a new career path, but it certainly felt like that.

It was a simple question that took away my internal debates and cemented my resolve. I asked myself if I could see myself in the same position in 10 years' time. The answer was clear. The thought of being stagnant and remaining at the same spot in 10 years' time gave me the chill. So I began my transition and the rest is a history.

From time to time in our life, we are no doubt faced with challenging decisions. The uncertainty that the future holds naturally contributes to our agony of indecisiveness. I have come to learn that there is one question that sets me free from indecisiveness when I stand at a cross road and that is the "10 years' time" question.

Not sure if you should change your job, ask yourself the "10 years' time" question – *what happens if I am still doing the same job in 10 years' time?*

Not sure if you should spend the money and send your children on a costly overseas exchange program with school, ask yourself the "10 years' time" question – *what happens if my children do not have the required cultural competency and global perspective in 10 years' time?*

There are no right or wrong answers. The "10 years' time" question is merely a tool to minimise the unhelpful internal debates happening inside our head when facing a challenging situation. Rather than continuing the indecisiveness, it is better to approach a difficult decision in a logical manner. The "10 years' time" question does exactly that.

It may be that you are comfortable with seeing yourself holding the same job in 10 years' time. Perhaps the job is close to home and gives you financial stability and that is okay as we all want different things in life.

Maybe you are not in a position to send your children on an expensive overseas exchange program with school, but recognising the importance of globalisation has on today's society, perhaps you could explore other affordable cultural experiences for your children.

Whatever our answers are, the "10 years' time" question gives us some confidence in our decision-making process. Therefore, do remember to ask yourself the question from time to time so you do not fall into the trap of indecisiveness and live to regret it.

Manoeuvre 2: Don't Fall Into The Trap Of Narrow-Minded Advice.

Part of my career transition was talking to recruitment agents and seeking their advice. One recruitment agent told me that my prospect of finding a decent position outside the medical field was not great. Her reasoning was based on the fact that my experience and skillsets up to this point were in a very niched area. In other words, by being specialised in the research area of blood vessel diseases meant that I was practically obsolete unless I remained in the scientific industry.

I thought that was absurd. The recruitment agent essentially was saying that one must be employed in the field of their chosen study. As I am a true believer that life is not a linear path but a convergent of my unexpected opportunities, I begged to differ.

So I thought about what other skills and experiences that I had that other industries apart from medicine would be interested in. I was glad the list was not a short one. In addition to my intellectual capacity and prior voluntary experience, I found others would appreciate my skills in general administration, project management and relationship building or even stakeholder engagement. All of these skills I applied during my time managing clinical research projects and these were the skillsets that my next employer valued the most.

Armed with my quiet self-confidence, I began the next phase of my career working as a project manager in the emergency management services sector. For the next 5 years, I had a lot of fun managing and delivering major projects that worth millions of dollars. It was also during this phase of my career that I experienced the strongest personal growth to date.

Had I listened to that well-meaning but narrow-minded recruitment agent, I would have never embarked on a journey of self-discovery and re-invention. So take people's advice seriously, but do so with caution so you do not fall into the trap of narrow-minded advice.

Manoeuvre 3: Don't Fall Into The Trap Of Linearity But Be The One Who Can Connect The Dots.

I was delivering a keynote speech to members of the Golden Key Honour Society. As the world's largest collegiate honour society who only invites the top 15% of university students to be members, it is suffice to say that I was talking to a group of academically gifted young people.

The focus of the keynote speech was about building an inclusive and resilient community as the organiser wished to make an emphasis on the fact that life is more than just good grades. Understanding the fact that life is not just one dimension and being able to put things in perspective, or even better, being able to "connect the dots" is a crucial skill to a young person.

This, of course, applies to all of us who may have graduated from university or college long ago.

What does it mean to be able to "connect the dots" and why is it so important to business success? "Connecting the dots" comes from one's ability to identify opportunities by making sense of a multitude of information, often from unlikely places. It requires an agile and open mind and it requires one to be flexible. "Connecting the dots" is a skill that many entrepreneurs or innovators possess and a skill that Steve Jobs used to describe about creativity.

So how does one learn to connect the dots? In addition to having an open mind, having as many diverse experiences as possible is crucial. It is extremely difficult to make sense of situations if one does not have enough knowledge or experience to draw on. A wide range of experiences provides a fertile ground where fresh and often unexpected ideas are born. This is one of the reasons why young people tend to think one dimension, because they have a lack of life experience.

To ensure that I do not exhaust my "knowledge or experience bank", I make sure that traveling is built into my business plan so I can continue to accrue new experiences. I particularly love to combine business and travel together, because it is cost and time effective. I also pay attention to "dig a little bit deeper" when I travel, so I am not just a tourist but a traveller who actually experiences.

For instance, through my many trips to Japan I have come to know Onigawara or ogre tile, a special type of roof ornament found in Japanese architecture that "protects" a home from evil. I have also met the last Oni-shi or ogre tile artisan in eastern Japan, Shigeru Yamaguchi.

Knowing Mr Yamaguchi, who is a 5th generation artisan keeping this dying art form alive, has got my mind working overtime. I ask myself: *What opportunities exist in this instance that local communities and my company can work on to save this dying art?* While ideas have just begun to surface, this particular travel experience demonstrates the importance of having a "knowledge or experience bank" on our ability to innovate and connect the dots.

To be successful, we need to remember that we do not live life in a linear fashion. So make sure to go out there and fill up our "bank" with a wide range of experiences. Go and live an enriched life!

Manoeuvre 4: Say No To The "Shotgun" Approach And Be Strategic About Your Growth And Development.

As an ambivert, I enjoy people's company and can function well in social setting, but very often I actually prefer to work alone. Given my slightly anti-social tendency, I have learned early on in my career to put strategies in place to ensure I do not become totally disengaged and live happily ever after by myself in my own bubble. So when it comes to setting a growth and development strategy, I make sure it is a very focused one.

For example, I sit on the governing board of 2 non-profit organisations. Being a company director provides me with governance training and career credibility, it also means that "I am out there" minimising my anti-social tendency. Further, to maintain my connection with the medical and health industry, one of the organisations that I hold a company directorship for is a community health organisation.

I also make sure that I deliver at least 2 public lectures or workshops every year. This is to ensure that I do not shy away from public speaking and as a non-native English speaker, I continue to provide myself opportunities to hone my language skills.

Having an understanding of myself and by being strategic about my growth and development, I have enjoyed many exciting opportunities made available to me. These opportunities include facilitating a Summit session at the United Nations Headquarters in New York City for a non-profit organisation and being invited to deliver a business lecture on innovation in Japan. Just like other aspects of our life, our growth and development strategy needs to be planned. Ideally, a growth and development plan that offers clarity has the following characteristics:

- It complements our long term goals.
- It addresses our areas of strengths by putting us slightly out of our comfort zone.
- It acts as a source of inspiration by giving us an opportunity to explore new things.

So one should take their time when it comes to planning for a growth and development strategy. Make sure the strategy takes a focused rather than a "shotgun" approach and covers the above mentioned characteristics.

With a strong growth and development strategy in place, we will not fall into the "shotgun" trap and will always be challenged in a positive way.

Manoeuvre 5: Don't Be The "Best-Kept Secret" And Make Sure To Curate Your Industry Credibility And Personal Brand Early.
I grew up in an encouraging and supportive culture where all children irrespective of their gender have an opportunity to flourish. But I also grew up in an Asian culture where humility is greatly valued. As a result, I have never felt truly comfortable in the lime light. One thing I had to learn in the early days of my career was to practise how to accept compliments.

As my career progresses, I made a decision to follow my entrepreneurial spirit and set up my own consulting firm. I loved my decision and have really embraced the freedom and intellectual challenges to undertake a wide variety of projects.

I also quickly learned that to succeed as a small business owner, you cannot be shy or be too humble. While we should not be outrageously boastful, we certainly should consider carefully curating a strategy that draws attention to ourselves in an elegant way. In other words, I had to learn how to curate my industry credibility and personal brand.

Part of being credible is to actually have real relevant experience under your belt, whether it is through formal academic study or life experience. For instance, a significant portion of my professional experience came from the public and non-profit sectors. I realised that I needed to gain some life experience to demonstrate my business acumen. I found my opportunity through chairing an "Innovation and Business Development" sub board committee for a community health organisation that is worth $15 million.

Curating industry authority and personal reputation also involves some savvy media and public relations skills. Learning the language of journalists and ways to discover the best angle to tell my stories were part of my media training journey.

Interestingly, I also had to learn to change my own mind-set when it came to the world of self-promotion. I had to learn to give myself permission to celebrate my success publicly and had to learn to speak about those successful stories to others and to media without feeling self-conscious.

So while being humble is still an important personal belief, I also understand the need to establish my industry credibility and personal brand. After all, it does not matter how good we are, if no one knows about us.

It is, therefore, incredibility important not to fall into the trap of being the "best-kept secret". Make sure to take required steps to build your industry credibility and personal brand in a positive way as early as possible in your career.

As I stood in front of my audience at the United Nations Headquarters in New York City, I thought to myself - *what an unexpected journey this has been.* When I started out many years ago as a medical scientist, I would have never thought one day that I would be visiting the United Nations Headquarters or being part of a team facilitating a global partnership summit.

Life is indeed unpredictable and forever changing, but it also offers endless opportunities for those who are ready to embrace them.

So make sure you are ready.

By Suzi Chen

Successful Women In Business – Leadership Edition

About The Author

Suzi Chen is a cross-disciplinary strategist who manages Notonos Global, an innovation driven business consulting firm that works with clients to "join the dots" and delivers successful business outcomes in an ethical and sustainable manner. The former medical scientist is also an award winning graphic designer, blog contributor and an avid traveller whose journey includes being a summit facilitator at the United National Headquarters in New York City in 2016.
Proud to be an enthusiastic dreamer, Suzi loves the fact that the world is full of possibilities and makes sure she is always challenged by new experiences.

This "forward-thinking" mind-set is reflected in Suzi's professional career, which spans across a wide range of industries including medical research, emergency management services and non-profit sector. Suzi believes in life-long learning and holds a doctoral degree in medical sciences and several other diplomas. Suzi sits on the company board of 2 non-profit organisations and chairs an Innovation and Business Development committee for a community health service provider.

To Find Out More Visit:

Website:
www.notonos.com

Twitter: @chensuzi

Email Suzi at shcen@notonos.com

From Nurse To Holistic Skin Specialist

"Your Purpose In Life Is To Find Your Purpose"

Gautama Buddha

As I loitered next to the oxygen cylinders a voice inside my head was calling out with increasing urgency: "Leave. Get out. Get out now." I had been working on the surgical ward at Bromley Hospital in the South East of England for a couple of years, and this had been a particularly busy and stressful shift. Added into the mix, the nursing manager I was working with had disappeared for a cigarette over an hour ago and still hadn't returned. This was when mobiles had just been born, so there were still only a few people who owned one. The next thing I knew, there was my nursing colleague and superior, being wheeled onto the ward in a hospital bed – she had gone for a fag and then admitted herself with suspected appendicitis, leaving me in charge of twenty-six very sick patients, and fuelling my secret suspicion that she had a case of the Munchausen's. (Needless to say her appendix was perfectly healthy).

That was it! This was the final push I needed to finally leave the NHS behind to pursue something alternative. I was fed up with being taken for granted, left in the lurch and told what to do, so knew I wanted to work for myself, but doing what? This was the olden days, when connecting to the Internet meant plugging a wire into the wall and listening to a strange extra-terrestrial dialling tone before Yahoo popped up on your screen. I spent hours researching possible career avenues, and soon realised that I had a real interest in alternative approaches to health.

By this time I had a young baby, so knew whatever I chose had to fit in with being a mum. When someone lent me a book about essential oils, I was enraptured and soon began experimenting on my family and around the home with different oils. The use of aromatics for healing purposes has been traced back to ancient Egypt, around 3500 BC. I was particularly interested in the fact that massaging different types of essential oils into the face and neck can bring about powerful responses in our skin. For example, many of us know that Tea Tree has antibacterial benefit, but I also learned that lesser known oils such as Fennel, Clary Sage and Wild Thyme are equally antiseptic. Essential oils - like many modern women - are multi-tasking, as their scents also have clinically proven benefits to the mind. Coming from a scientific background, I am always keen to ensure that these aromatherapy-type claims have clinical research to back them up, and I am never disappointed. For example, a trial involving 79 college students with sleep disorders reported better sleep patterns and awaking feeling refreshed after just 5 nights of inhaling Lavender essential oil(*). In addition, the benefits were still going strong two weeks post-trial when the subjects were followed up. Another study proved that inhaling Ginger essential oil during chemotherapy treatment significantly reduces nausea and vomiting, and improves appetite**.

In terms of skincare, numerous trials have looked at the benefit of essential oil application to adult and child eczema, dermatitis and dry skin. One such trial showed that a blend of Lavender and Tea Tree oils had an immediate effect by soothing itching***, and several studies carried out on Rose, Helichrysum and Bergamot essential oils have highlighted that these botanical extracts have powerful antioxidant benefit, meaning that they are able to protect our skin from free radicals. ****

Completely sold on the supreme benefit this therapy could impart to my future customers, I enrolled on a Clinical Aromatherapy course. This qualification meant I could eventually help people sort out the root cause of their health issues, rather than just the symptoms.

I decided to do an extra module to learn how essential oils can be used to exert their unique benefits onto skin, both through direct application as well as inhaling their scents.

From the moment I started my course in London, I absolutely loved it – this felt so right and I was immediately fascinated – still am - by the power and benefit of essential oils; truly a gift from nature. I clearly remember my first day when I made a simple blend of Lavender and Patchouli, and a fellow classmate massaged it into my shoulders. I felt heady, completely relaxed and I was hooked. The great thing with scents is that they jog memories, and I am always transported back to that day every time I work with these specific essential oils.

I met a lovely lady on the course, Sara, and by the time we'd qualified, had decided to team up to help each other out. Sara had an existing client base because she owned a clinic and she began referring her clients to me, and vice versa. This became the first lesson I learned about business: three to the power of two – meaning, there is true strength in collaborating with others of similar mind sets, in helping each other and creating a strong story together.

It was 2000 and very quickly I had a small group of clients I was working closely with on various health issues, yet they all had one thing in common – imbalanced skin. Some of the imbalances seemed insignificant on the surface in that they were easy to treat – dryness or dehydration for example – but I became aware that I could only do so much healing through the use of essential oils and Aromatherapy alone. As I delved deeper into the realms of these clients' lifestyles, I realised that stress, poor diet and sleep patterns (to name a few), also play a huge role in our skin's condition and wellbeing.

Enter business lesson number two: adapting to your client's needs equals wonderful customer service. If you do something new for your clients, they feel special, and they are more likely to remain loyal, (plus it makes you feel all fuzzy inside). So, I decided to add to my skill set by doing a course in Skin Nutrition – how to nourish skin from the inside out through diet and care of the gut. I developed the practice of promoting good gut circulation alongside a realistic dietary routine for my clients, because so many people have poor gut absorption, meaning they gain zero benefit from eating the right foods, however many supplements they take or platefuls of kale they might consume.

I also began making bespoke skincare for my customers at this point – natural, organic facial oils, creams and balms designed and tailor-made for their skin and mind. They could even select a preferred type of scent – whether they preferred woody, fresh, calming or floral base notes. Often I would infuse products with raw juice from herbs and flowers such as parsley, sage and tamarind, or tea extracts such as Rose Hip and Fennel to make the skincare as fresh as possible, and I was literally making everything from home on the work surfaces in my kitchen, frequently at night once the children were in bed.

This led to my third and fourth business lessons: create a niche for yourself in a crowded market and let your work speak for itself. There were lots of other Clinical Aromatherapists around at the time, but I was coming from a fresh angle. My clients were happy, and word was spreading. I was also formulating tailor-made blends for the body; one client had lymphatic oedema in her right arm following a right mastectomy. She was very self-conscious of her swollen arm, felt that people were staring at her when she was in company and that it was a tell-tale sign of her former illness.

I had cared for lots of mastectomy patients as a nurse, and knew this was a very common problem following breast surgery as there are some great, whopping lymphatic drainage ducts in the upper body, which become imbalanced through the surgery, meaning that drainage becomes difficult. For this lady, I suggested a combination of regular lymphatic drainage massage and an essential oil blend to promote good blood flow through her arm, shoulders and thorax (chest). I chose Geranium, Oregano, Rosemary and Lemon, which all work to encourage blood flow in the body and so oxygen supply to the tissues. These are also naturally detoxifying, cleansing oils to purify skin and blood, which smell gorgeous and have a similar boosting effect on the mind.

The lady came to see me once weekly and we used her oil to massage over these areas, plus she continued this at home three more times every week. The results were astounding - she was wearing short sleeves again within a month and crucially, her confidence and self-esteem soared.

I also had many male clients with all sorts of skin issues. I recall the first time I saw one gentleman in particular who originally came to see me about his adult acne; well actually, he had suffered with back acne since he was a teenager but he now had cystic acne to the mid and lower face. When I see a client for the first time, I am often assessing them for what they are *not* saying; subtle body movements for instance, how they dress, their posture, and so on. This was a leftover nursing skill, picked up through years of reviewing new patients. The man was dressed entirely in black. It was a sunny day and he wore a hat with a huge brim pulled down over his eyes. He also covered his mouth a lot when he spoke. In short, I could see that he was agonisingly self-conscious about his skin, and it was dramatically affecting his everyday life.

I developed a programme for him, providing him with recipes to make his own daily face masks at home using edible ingredients, (giving him autonomy over his treatment), whilst making him a range of bespoke skincare products containing raw, natural and organic extracts, plus weekly aromatherapy treatments. I also referred him for stomach acid assessment and designed a dietary programme, including foods high in antioxidants and low in wheat, dairy and GM ingredients. I advised him to swap all of his household cleaning, shaving products and fragrance for plant-based ones. The products I made for him were designed to balance his skin and uplift his spirit, and included an essential oil blend of Sweet Orange, Chamomile, Ledum and Sandalwood to support the nervous system and liver. He was able to burn the blends around the home, as well as apply to his pulse points throughout the day. His acne quickly changed to a non-inflammatory form and he was delighted. I worked closely with this client over many years and he has become a close friend.

After 5 or so years, I had a waiting list of clients. I had three children by now and wasn't always able to meet demand. Sometimes I drove out to clients' homes to see them in the evenings, which was hard when I might not have slept much the night before, or if one of the boys was poorly, but my passion for and belief in my business always spurred me on. In 2012 my business was 12 years old, and I was seeing clients from all over the UK and Europe too. Until now, much of my work had been 'underground' – I hadn't invested in exotic advertising or PR, relying on word of mouth only. I felt ready to take the business to the next level and the first thing I decided to do was set up a proper skincare brand, based on blends I had used with my clients, who provided me with an existing customer base. Although I was able to use the lessons I had learned from the Aromatherapy business, I soon realised this was a slightly different ball game.

Skincare is what I would describe as fiddly – packaging design, labelling, the product inside and the presentation must all come together beautifully and quite often, even with the best intentions, it simply doesn't work so you have to scrap everything and start over. I remember spending an entire Sunday evening trying to put a new roll of labels onto some glass bottles I had invested in. Each time I applied one, unsightly bubbles would form over the surface and the labels would crease up. After a few hours of approaching this supposedly simple task through many different methods, I was so hot, frustrated and close to tears that I had to admit defeat. I later learned that this was because the labels were made out of paper, which is always difficult to apply.

During an early London launch of the skincare business, my PR lady had to stop me from unpacking boxes of products in front of the journalists; I was so used to being hands-on I didn't realise that this was not the done thing within the world of beauty. And of course the thought of speaking to the editors and bloggers present made me quiver, but I reminded myself to be authentic and allow my passion for my business to come through. On several occasions I dispatched orders to clients, who then e-mailed me to tell me something had leaked or everything was smashed when it arrived, so I would have to spend time re-making the products and dispatching them all over again. Yes, getting the skincare brand, which I named Inner-Soul Organics - off the ground took a lot of mental strength on a daily basis, and I had to watch where every penny went like a hawk, as I was self-funding.

To save on costs, I built my own website initially which took me a total of nine months, and sourced packaging and ingredients in small quantities. I also formulated everything myself and found an independent chemist's apprentice to do all the product safety testing. My brilliant designer Mike, and London-based manufacturer, Steve, helped to make it all a lot smoother and I launched a small range for face, bath and body in the August of 2012, all created using fresh, organic plant extracts.

The global skincare market was worth around 96 billion USD in 2012, and today has grown to 121 billion USD, so it was of utmost importance that I stuck to my business lesson number three, creating something to set me apart from other skincare brands. Inner-Soul Organics products are made in small batches, often fresh to order, using raw, antioxidant extracts with proven skin benefit.

The brand today offers seventeen products across face, bath and body, plus unisex, Mum and Baby, Nordic-Inspired and Bespoke options, and won its first skincare award within the first few months of trading. I have employed a lovely part-time publicist in-house and the brand appears regularly in respectable press, plus I contribute to various magazines, including The Peridot Mag and www.getthegloss.com. We have won several more awards in spite of being a small company, and this past year have tripled our turnover.

This process has taught me my fifth business lesson: stay focused on what you believe in. It sounds obvious, maybe a little cheesy, but I have often repeated this mantra to myself over the years, especially when things get tricky.

I sometimes imagine I'm on a path, and look at what is at the end of the path for my current business goal, which might be a product launch or a new supplier. If I want something, I visualise myself having it, and implicitly trust my own judgment. I also try to treat others how I wish to be treated and never promise to deliver something I can't.

My career journey has taken me from the vocational to the commercial and it's been a huge learning curve. But at night when it's quiet, I still think about those oxygen cylinders and how they led me to build a fulfilling and fascinating business, which I dearly love.

By Emma Coleman

REFERENCES:

*Effect of Inhaled Lavender and Sleep Hygiene on Self-Reported Sleep Issues: A Randomized Controlled Trial. Lillehei AS et al

** Effects of inhaled ginger aromatherapy on chemotherapy-induced nausea and vomiting and health-related quality of life in women with breast cancer. Lua PL et al

*** Case History of Infected Eczema Treated with Essential Oils, C. Blamey et al

**** Biological properties and resistance reversal effect of Helichrysum italicum (Roth) G. Don E. Guinoiseau et al; Antioxidant Activities and Volatile Constituents of Various Essential Oils, Alfreda Wei and Takayuki Shibamoto

About The Author

Emma started off as a nurse (NHS) in the 90's before qualifying as a Clinical Aromatherapist in 2000 specialising in her passion, care of the skin. After subsequently taking a course in Skin Nutrition, she worked closely with clients, creating tailor-made programmes to balance their various skin issues with a unique, holistic approach through education, and tailor-made natural and organic skincare routines and dietary input.
Her services grew through word of mouth as the results were so visual, she launched her own skincare brand Inner-Soul Organics – available at

Successful Women In Business – Leadership Edition

www.inner-soul.co.uk - in 2012 using raw, antioxidant ingredients to protect and nourish skin. Emma still formulates and designs every product in the award-winning ranges today and continues to work with a few clients and their families throughout the UK and Europe.

Emma says, "As well as loving the process of designing and creating products and holistic skin programmes, I passionately believe each skin type is individual to us and factors such as lifestyle, natural sleep pattern, diet and personality must be considered. Therefore, each of my clients is viewed as unique – one-size-fits-all simply doesn't work in sorting out skin issues."

Many of the products in the Inner-Soul Organics range are based on tailor-made skincare designed for Emma's former clients; for example Circulation Boost Skin Oil is based on a massage product originally formulated for a lady who, following a mastectomy, had developed Lymph oedema to her left arm. Inner-Soul Organics offers freshly made skincare products from anti-ageing, unisex to pregnancy-friendly, plus individually created bespoke products.

To Find Out More Visit:

E-mail: emma@inner-soul.co.uk

Instagram: InnerSoulOrganicsSkincare

Facebook: InnerSoulOrganics

Twitter: @EmmaInnerSoul

YouTube: InnerSoulOrganicsTV

Building More Than Just a Salon

Hairdressing was not ultimately what I wanted to do as a career, when I was at school I first wanted to be a ballerina. I eventually grew out of that notion and my ambition switched to being accepted at Glasgow School of Art. Whilst studying I applied for a Saturday job for a salon group called Irvine Rusk, who at that time had a growing reputation in Glasgow for being an up and coming name in hairdressing.

A friend informed me that I would have to be able to shampoo hair and would possibly be asked to demonstrate this at my interview. I practiced on anyone that would let me try for a week before and was hugely disappointed that this was not part of a Saturday girl interviewing process.

I just loved the job, dealing with the public and being creative at the same time. What really appealed to me was the glamorous side to our industry, as Irvine Rusk were part of a new generation that were producing creative photographic work, taking part in shows and seminars and working as platform artists on stage. Scottish hairdressing was gaining a reputation for being one of the best in the world, this combined with an awareness of current clothes fashion, art and interior design.

It appealed to both the artist and ballerina inside me, so I decided then and there that this was the career choice for me. I did not return to school and started my full time training and at sixteen I knew I would one day have my own business.

In 1982 I took the opportunity to change job and started working with Alan Stewart (now my husband), who had opened a 2,500 square foot salon in the heart of Glasgow's city centre. He had previously been a partner/art director with Irvine but had decided to follow his own destiny. He had a strong vision of how he would like a salon environment to be and the type of company he would like to run.

Successful Women In Business – Leadership Edition

The salon was quite radical to all other salons in Glasgow, one because of its size but also his concept of giving clients a bespoke service, longer appointment times, in-depth consultations, luxury products, advanced colouring techniques and charging premium prices. He also was very involved in education, hair shows, seminars producing photographic work for magazines and he was looking for an artistic team to work alongside him. I then had the opportunity to explore the creative side in me and loved creating avant-garde hair for shows, learning how to style hair for photographs, innovating new haircutting, colour and perming techniques and demonstrating them either on stage or in the classroom. This totally consumed me. We would work for nine hours in the salon working on our clients then would practice at night on models, wigs, concepts, and we even hired a tutor to help us with public speaking, videoing ourselves on stage then critiquing our performance. We had very limited resources then, so my dancing experience was put to good use choreographing presentations and Alan and I learned how to apply make up for stage and camera.

I also became the PR for the salon and wrote press releases and mailed out information and photographs to all the UK and international hair publications. We also produced a series of 20 educational video tapes based on our cutting techniques. All of this effort started to pay off, as we were in demand to perform in the USA, Australia, South Africa and Europe and took part in major trade events in the UK. It sounds very glamorous but we were still on very limited budgets, when we were demonstrating at the London trade shows, both the team and the models accompanying us travelled down on public transport (overnight bus) sometimes without even a seat, and I would have made packed lunches for all.

We often had groups of foreign students coming to Glasgow to learn from us, and we needed more space to be able to facilitate the education arm of the business, so an opportunity arose in 1984 to buy a salon that was prime site, a couple of hundred yards from the flagship salon.

This was a salon that Alan had previously managed for another company, and he had made it a huge success in its time but now the owners wanted to retire. Alan opened this opportunity up to the art directors working for him, and wanted a commitment and large deposit to make one of us a partner in the business. The new salon would be predominantly a hairdressing education facility with a small salon attached. This was the opportunity I was looking for and the next day I put my flat on the market to raise the capital.

We had major plans for the space, which included the latest interior design, which did not come cheap. We also had a substantial bank loan to fund the project. Having your own business is a steep learning curve, I was having to learn a new set of skills as we did not have the resources to employ a team. My duties included, opening and closing the salon, cashing up daily, writing hand financial and stylist trend reports, bookkeeping, paying wages on Kalamazoo weekly,(this also entailed going to the bank and getting the exact cash amounts to put in envelopes) filing VAT returns, stock procurement, ordering/taking, daily management/running the business, dealing with quality control, hiring and firing, training the team, running an advanced training academy, bookings, course planning and teaching. Now we have a team, and work with agencies that specialise in their field, but the beauty of starting off so lean, and developing the business as a team, is that there is not a job that someone does for us now that we do not know how to do or have done.

We were quite naïve then and did not have a plan B, if we did not fill our school up every week with foreign students. We thought "if you build it, they will come". Our jolly bank manager changed and Alan and I received a call from our new bank manager who forcibly pointed out that we were spending more weekly than we were bringing in. We were continuing to travel the world and not really getting paid enough for the time effort and money we were spending pursuing this avenue, coupled with not enough students and a small hairdressing staff. He told us it all had to change, with immediate effect and if we did not bring in more money this week he would not pay the staffs wages. This was the biggest wakeup call we ever got. We honestly thought we were going to lose not just one salon but both salons and if he were to decide to retract the loan we would also lose our homes. We had been working as hard as we could with the ultimate goal to create a reputation for producing and teaching the best in our craft, and making money was the last thing on our agenda.

We did not go to bed that night and poured over the figures, how could we save money and how could we increase our turnover. The figures kept coming back with the same sum, we would have to double our turnover/number of clients and number of staff within a week. This was just not possible, then we looked at it from a different angle it was the profit we needed not the turnover, so a plan was hatched, we would sell two day seminars to all the local salons, and do these on a Sunday and Monday, we enlisted a local rep from a salon suppliers and paid him a commission on every seminar he sold. We had worked out if we could get ten people per two days, for a few weeks this would give us the reprieve we needed. Then we could work on increasing the salon staff and clientele.

It was a shock to us that this rep came back and said he has sold sixty tickets and could we give him more dates as he could sell the same again. We also at that time abandoned the idea of an advanced Academy and focused on training our own people. It took us eighteen months to completely turn the business around. We worked seven days a week, as many hours as it took. Not long after we had got everything back on track we received an invitation to the boardroom from the bank manager, to attend a four course lunch to celebrate the success of our business, I can remember whispering to Alan, do you think there is some poor business owner downstairs, being told the bank will not pay their wages?

When we started we were working on a vision and a passion but coming so close to losing everything, I changed my focus and I remember saying to Alan, I no longer want to be recognised for being the best hairdresser but for being the best business woman in the industry. We then became business junkies, attending business seminars, reading every book we could find, attended motivational courses and at night watched videos relating to business, coaching, and self-development and in the car always had a tape in the cassette. Alan started as my business partner and through our shared vision and passion for learning, we eventually became a couple.

We also took the opportunity to take a major step in 1990 and purchased a 6,000 square foot, five story building on the opposite side of the square from the second salon, we needed more space to educate our growing team and had decided to add beauty to our services. Anyone from the outside looking in would scratch there head as to why we would open three large salons within a few hundred yards from each other? When we opened the second salon, the first did not lose any new business, and through developing people both businesses grew, so we applied the same principal to the third and it was a success. This meant that we dominated the Glasgow city centre market.

With all this newfound knowledge, we implemented structure, systems, ideas, to both our business and team, continually imparting our knowledge on the team. This resulted in our team growing in size, knowledge, ability and nurturing and developing them as both hairdressers and individuals, working on developing their strengths. This then resulted in producing a really strong team who all were like minded and wanted to be part of our growing business who had bought in to our values and culture. I worked on a ten year plan, with education being the mainstay and worked on how we could evolve and how the team could be part of it. We decided to go down the route of franchising the business, this would allow us to benefit but the individual would have the opportunity to be in control of their own income and benefit from the work they put in. We only franchise to our own people, who know and understand the brand and standards. We also developed our own product range to reflect our philosophy on working with the best hair condition. We have a policy for sustainable organic growth in all avenues of the business and have underpinned the business with the property arm and where possible have purchased most of the salon properties.

We have at present twelve salons, making us the largest, both in size and staff numbers salon group in Scotland. Not only have the salons grown but so has the education arm of our business. We eventually opened a standalone school in 2002, but quickly grew out of the space and in 2006 opened a 7,500sq foot state of the art academy in Glasgow. We have won many awards for our education and a recent HMI report gave us four excellent score. We were also filmed for over a year for BBC Scotland and starred in a four part documentary following the career of ten brand new trainees.

We also nurtured a team to work on the artistic side of the business and they continue to show the Rainbow Room International brand of hairdressing and are ambassadors for the company. We have a team who work on events, T in the Park, Baftas, Mobos etc. and have styled many celebrities and stars.

We had many other challenges along the way, our second salon was flooded from the offices above and we did not realise we were under insured and had to use all of our wits to keep the business afloat. We had to manage the situation because it was a listed building, due to the restrictions we had to let it dry our naturally, which took a year. We moved in to the other salon across the road - this did lose us clients and suppressed the growth of both salons during this period. When we bought the building in Royal Exchange Square, even although we had four different types of surveys, when work started, the floors would not take the load capacity and we ended up in the basement looking at the roof.

Our industry is a vibrant creative one and it gives you the opportunity to become anything you want, an artist, teacher, manager, salon owner, but it does take hard work and dedication. I still have a few clients that I like to do their hair. It is the clients that keep the job interesting. They come from many walks of life and have extended knowledge of all subjects. I feel that you have to keep growing, learning and never be afraid to make mistakes or take chances. I always say to our team, unless you are taking calculated risks and pushing forward, the minute you step off the path and just try to hang on to what you have got, then it is a slippery road to going backwards. During the recession of 2008 we stepped up and increased the education of the team, put the focus on taking our service to new levels instead of trying to cut back.

We have succeeded by always trying to be the best, first or different. Sometimes not all of our ideas have worked, but the team expect change, although it is slightly more difficult the bigger we get to turn the whole ship round overnight, but we are always open to new ideas. We have communication on all levels, as head office is in the Academy we see all the trainees on a weekly basis, and the whole team have to attend at least four advanced training courses a year. Alan and I personally run consultation, team building, and management and train the trainer courses, throughout the year. We also have senior management meetings every four weeks.

We have our level of success though the synergy of the team work, have management teams, training teams, blog squad, artistic teams, and reception teams, and bring people together to improve systems and quality. Each year, for the past 30 years, we come together for a Staff Congress. The first one was very small, giving out crystal glasses as prizes and a day conference with on overhead projector. It has grown into a full day conference, which guest speakers, hair show and a glittering awards dinner art night. Our pay system factors in annual bonuses and in 2016 we gave out £60,000 in bonus cheques. We have many categories in our personalised RRI awards. The more prestigious awards are given for continual improvement. This is a system we adopted 30 years ago after a visit to Japan, to encourage small continual improvements. The night is always a great testament to the team work of the company, although the salons do compete with each other, they all celebrate each other's achievements.

We are aware that future clients are very different and we have to keep up with technology, we have put a major focus on managing our social media and using a media agency who work closely with our PR agency. It is another skill set that we need to learn, but it is important to keep up with all the technology, we realised that on-line was growing and 18 years ago we commissioned a computer developer to write our own on line booking/salon management programme. This was again another of life's experiences, the budget started at £30,000.

At the time, there was not a live booking systems for clients (book and get an E Mail Back) the first company folded and another company took over and between the two companies it ended up costing ten times original cost. We have built up a very recognisable brand, and by some we are referred to as an institution. This has been achieved through dedication, hard work and a passion for educating others and ourselves, not being afraid to fail and being innovative.

By Linda Stewart

About The Author

Rainbow Room International are Scotland's most successful hairdressing and beauty salon group, with twelve award-winning salons throughout the country they are regarded throughout the global hairdressing industry as leaders and innovators.

Rainbow Room International are passionate about education and already have their very own training academy and fame academy within Glasgow city centre. Their Academy of Hair situated at 64 Howard Street, Glasgow is one of the largest in Europe and confirmed Rainbow Room International as one of Europe's leading hairdressing brands.

With a floor area of 7,500 sq ft dedicated to student development, this state of the art academy of hair has opened the way for candidates throughout the UK, to learn and achieve qualifications such as NVQ 2/3 and Modern Apprenticeships as students at the forefront of today's most advanced development programme.

As well as being a centre of education for the Rainbow Room International team, the academy is open to non Rainbow Room International staff and attracts many hairdressers from the UK and overseas. The academy has its own inspirational training prospectus of courses running and also acts as a Schwarzkopf centre of education offering Schwarzkopf ASK courses.

Rainbow Room International's Academy of Hair provides highly motivated professional coaches, all of whom gained their knowledge and experience within the renowned Rainbow Room international education and training system. The student learning programme utilises fully integrated video, DVD, and online technologies as part of the theory development, and, in addition to the vast experience available to students through the Rainbow Room International group, students are regularly exposed to motivational demonstrations by the highly acclaimed Rainbow Room International Art Team.

This outstanding facility compliments many years' experience in the development of techniques for early student training and beyond to advanced and creative styling techniques.

Rainbow Room had commissioned a gallery of hands from the most creative and motivating hairdressers including Vidal Sassoon, Trevor Sorbie, Annie Humphreys, Tim Hartley and Luis Llongueras.

Rainbow Room International directors Alan and Linda Stewart are extremely proud of Academy of Hair; "The reason behind the opening of the academy was that we needed premises large enough to cope with 100 trainees a day for our company plans. Once we found suitable premises it was down to creating a space that young trainees and hairdressers from across the globe would like to come and work within. It had to be a world class training centre, be easy to manage and have multi-usable spaces/studios that could be changed from lecture theatre style to salon to photographic studio with minimal disruption and as quickly as possible.

Throughout the development of the academy a lot of custom building was required but well worth it to achieve the concept successfully. We did not want to lose the immense feeling of space so we used a considerable amount of glass to keep the open and airy feeling. It also allows our head of training to monitor where everyone is and how courses are progressing at any time during the day.

The academy has already allowed us to work more efficiently and is a fantastic environment to work in. The academy has increased the number of internal and external students learning within Rainbow Room International and we are delighted with the project and the standards that are being achieved."

        Rainbow Room International Academy of Hair
        64 Howard Street, Glasgow, G1 4EE
        Tel: 0141 221 0400

        www.rainbowroominternational.com

Success: Profit Or Purpose And Personal Fulfilment?

Introduction

Thesaurus: Synonym of Success - Prosperity

"Prosperity doesn't mean that you will have wealth, health and happiness. The best way to explain prosperity is to say it is like when a rosebud flowers and opens up, and it shares its fragrance. That's the moment, which lasts a few days, when a rose flower is prosperous. When a man or woman is prosperous, it is the fragrance of security, grace, depth, character, and truthfulness that a person can share. Like a candle emits light, a human emits prosperity."

A quote from Yogi Bhajan, the Founder of Kundalini Yoga 12/26/97 from

"Success and the Spirit: An Aquarian Path to Prosperity"

What Is Success?

From a young age we are programmed to think of success in monetary terms, in terms of wealth and financial prosperity. We are accustomed to think that a CEO of a Corporation or a Self-Made Millionaire has achieved more success than we have because they have gained position, influence and affluence.

At school we strive for the best exam results; not only in Australia but all around the world, students sit for their final high school certificate (High School Certificate or equivalent) at aged 17/18; the results that arrive in an envelope at the end of their education is considered the reflection of their entire school career and define how successful they have been.

After school many of us will aim for the best university to study for the best course that will get us the best career. We'll want the best job that will lead us to the best promotion and the highest salary. We'll want the best partner, the best house in the best street. We'll then repeat the cycle through our kids hoping they'll achieve more than we did. This is how we measure our success.

There is nothing wrong with any of this provided we don't lose sight of the end goal. That end goal has to be personal fulfilment and a life of contentment. That is true success. Easier said than done one might assume, but if we go within ourselves to discover our life's purpose then the end goal will be within our grasp.

It would be fascinating to survey CEOs of top corporations as to whether they feel have reached a level of success or whether they are continually striving to reach that level. In their search for success are they in fact working such long hours at the detriment of everything else in their life that real success will never be theirs?

It is time we measured success in different terms – in terms of fulfilment through your work and in terms of finding joy in what you do. Let's talk about a successful business owner as one whose mission is to make a positive change in the world, be it within their community or even on a global level.

We generally believe a company to be successful if it has achieved profitability and growth. But how often does a corporation achieve that success, without consciously considering its company ethos and culture amongst its staff? How often do corporations take from staff, suppliers and even their customers in search of that bottom line profit margin but give very little back? A truly successful company is one that recognizes the value of partnerships with its suppliers, staff and customer base, not one that exists solely for soaring profit margins. In the world of retail, there is a growing movement away from fast fashion and an industry that has profited from the spoils of factory slave labour to achieve its success. Conscious Consumerism is a flourishing trend that is prompting major retailers to develop ethical practices and to invest in sustainable production methods. This has been the background to the creation of Temples and Markets, an online store I founded in early 2015. I wanted to create a business that provided an enjoyable buying experience at every point for the customer; one that provides the customer with the added halo effect that when they shop they are doing some good in the global community. It is in essence what I call the Win-Win effect.

The measure of success for my business is two-fold. It provides a win-win for the customer but for the suppliers too. The core value is that the suppliers – Artisan Groups, Emerging Designers and Social Enterprise whose creations I showcase in store – share in its achievements. Their stories are told on the website bringing them closer to the consumer in a way that is rare in the often cold world of E-commerce.

My Story:

So many of us, meander through life from one job to another or from one business to another striving to find our life's purpose. It may have been staring us in the face for a long time but fear or self-doubt prevented us from grabbing it. And so it was with me.

From a very young age I knew, as corny as it sounds, that I wanted to make a difference. Having studied history at university and being a staunch humanitarian, I am often affected emotionally by the world's injustices. During university I dreamed of doing something worthwhile with my life, but as a graduate in London in the late 80s I just had to find a job. I found myself in the cutthroat world of chain store buying and merchandising, not many opportunities to make a difference in the world there. Although I worked up the ladder, I was pleased to turn my back on that life when I left the U.K in 1997 to travel the world.

I spent 5 months trekking the well-worn backpacking path of some of S.E Asia's most visited countries. It was during that trip that I expanded my knowledge of how hard the world is and in contrast, how charmed my life is. The region found its way into my heart and has never left. Since that first trip I have returned to Thailand, Indonesia, Malaysia, China, Hong Kong and Singapore, Vietnam and Laos many times.

It would be reasonable to say I'm addicted to travelling, shopping and eating my way through South East Asia and get back there as often as I can. The region is so full of contrasts – from the buzz of the night markets to the serenity of a resort spa, from a visit to an ancient Buddhist temple followed by a ride in a Tuk-Tuk through noisy bustling streets. I love the smells of Lemongrass and Frangipani and the tastes of hot curries and tropical fruit. I love eating noodle soup for breakfast and satay sticks by a pool.

Most of all, lingering memories from travelling in S.E Asia have come from the gracious and warm people I've met along the way. I have never failed to be awestruck by the resilience, strength and astounding creativity of the people I spent time getting to know. In countries such as Vietnam and Cambodia, where recent history has caused great hardships, horror seems to have begat beauty. Much has happened in those 20 years since I first backpacked through South East Asia. During that trip it became clear that on returning to the rat race life in London was never going to be an option and I migrated to Sydney, Australia.

Frequent travel, motherhood and a brush with the real possibility of an early demise in the form of breast cancer at the age of 36 have shaped who I am today. Cancer was simultaneously the best and worst thing to have happened to me. Ten years on I live with the real possibility of a recurrence but with life so short I am more conscious of a desire for fulfilment, positivity and contentment.

I tried the corporate world for a few years in advertising but I don't have the make up to work for somebody else. I have a fierce independent entrepreneurial streak and a creative personality. Furthermore, to avoid a cancer recurrence, I was determined to avoid stress where possible and instead follow a regime of daily exercise and an organic diet. After my recovery I looked for a creative outlet whereby I could fulfil my own destiny. I'd always had an interest in interior design and formed an Interior Design and Project Management company. Doesn't that sound like a glamorous and creative existence? Or perhaps you're reading this and have experience of the building industry and you're probably laughing at the idea, that I thought I'd avoid stress in that world. And you'd be right to be laughing. I'm laughing now at the thought of it. I literally believed I could make a difference in this male dominated arena; even act as a client advocate when it came to negotiating on their behalf with tradespeople. In reality the only positivity I got out of that life was at the end of a project; it was always a delight to see a transformation of a property that I'd played a part in creating. But the path to getting there was never without its battles and upsets.

Suffice to say it took a long time to realize that the path to success lay in recognising and following my passion. Everything that came prior, be it illness or failure in business, was part of the journey to get me to that point. If I was to achieve success in terms of fulfilment, the timing had to be right. In early 2015 the catalyst presented itself and the concept of Temples and Markets, an idea that had been milling around in my mind for a long while, came to fruition.

Temples And Markets

During a trip to Siem Reap in Cambodia in January 2015, I stumbled upon a small boutique selling handmade jewellery. Had I not been dining at a café in the same laneway as the boutique, chances are I would never have come across it. The window display was striking – bold and contemporary jewellery pieces fashioned from local seeds such as I'd never seen before. I was drawn in and learnt the story behind the jewellery and the designer, Rany, who created the pieces. She became the impetus for Temples and Markets.

> *Rany returned to Siem Reap after a failed marriage in India. She'd been away for 4 years. Sadly her parents didn't approve of divorce and she wasn't welcomed back into the family home.*
>
> *Times were tough and Rany struggled to find work. She'd always been creative but as the oldest of 7 kids had never had the opportunity to go to design or art school. She saw potential in the small, colourful seeds on the road in Siem Reap and collected some, determined to turn them into something beautiful. It took time to work out how to make holes in the seeds; she borrowed a drill and cut her hands. She persevered though and made her first pair of earrings followed by a small collection that she shared with her friends. They were impressed and urged her to make*

more.

Fast-forward to today and she now has 7 local women handcrafting the beautiful jewellery she designs in the small workshop behind her boutique. I've watched them, sitting cross-legged on the floor, drilling into every tiny seed with meticulous care.

Selecting the seeds is a painstaking process - each has to be the perfect size, shape and symmetry to fit with her designs. Rany used to collect them herself; now the local villagers collect them for her.

I'd heard so many stories in S.E Asia like Rany's, of survival spawning creativity and success. The time was right to bring these stories to an audience outside the region. By telling their stories via an online store that showcases their creations, I have developed a platform that literally helps trade artisans and emerging designers, often marginalised or from poverty stricken communities, into a better life.

I already knew there was a market for unique finds from my travels. After previous trips to Thailand or Vietnam I'd come back wearing a piece of jewellery or a bag and repeatedly be asked, "Where did you get that?" I'd watch the enquirer's face drop when I told them "that comes from Thailand and isn't available in Australia". An idea formulated in my mind that I should give my fabulous finds access to a market outside of S.E Asia and expose the emerging designers and artisan groups I met to a wider audience outside of the region.

I should add that when I'd returned from travelling I'd often reminisce about the myriad of creations I'd seen and regretted not buying for reasons of budget or luggage space. I was aware that this affliction was exclusively mine and that there'd be a market of other travellers who'd also returned home from S.E Asia with what I call "Buyers Regret." In November 2015 the online store Temples and Markets went live. It was a year in the making – sourcing products, designing the website, product photography and copy writing, which saw me working into the early hours for weeks on end in the run up

Successful Women In Business – Leadership Edition

to launch. But I wouldn't have had it any other way. This was my baby and I felt immense pride in how it turned out and the positive feedback it received. Visitors to the site early on were surprised at the wide range of exquisite and unique products available. Perhaps they were expecting cheapie souvenir type merchandise that we all know is found all over Thai or Vietnamese markets. On the contrary, Temples and Markets show cases pieces across its collections that have a clear designer element to them. Within a few short months Temples and Markets evolved, initially the concept had been to expose emerging designers and artisans with that oriental twist to a larger audience outside of the region.

Quickly it became increasingly about affecting positive change in the region that I love. I added Social Enterprises such as the *Senhoa Foundation* whose tagline is "Employ, Empower, Emancipate" Proceeds from the sales of exquisite Senhoa Jewellery go directly to the rehabilitation and education of young women who are vulnerable to or are survivors of slavery in Cambodia. I added *Smateri*a, founded by two Italian designers who had two very clear objectives: to create a beautiful, high-quality product using 'bizarre' materials, and to employ Cambodian workers in a fair and sustainable way, giving priority to women and mothers. Their stylist bags are fashioned from recycled fishing nets or leather sofa offcuts.

Zsiska Jewellery was always going to be featured in the store; their colourful vibrant necklaces I'd been wearing for years had been the subject of many a "Where did you get that" enquiries. Dutch designer Siska founded her namesake company in 1992 in Cha-Am near Bangkok. The fourteen women with whom Siska started the company still work for Zsiska today. It is a family affair with most of their family members and children joining the company to work in a social environment.

It didn't take long for other Social Organisations, who fit within the premise of Temples and Markets, to approach me for inclusion. I've been only too delighted to support them and so proud that they'd heard about my work and its purpose. Orphaned during the horror days of Cambodia's Khmer Rouge, Chanta Theon heads up *Angkor Bullet Jewellery*, a group of home-based artisans, some vulnerable and disabled, who reside in a small community around 30 minutes from Phnom Penh. Decided they would transform bullet casings, a symbol of war, into unique designer jewellery. From horror comes beauty.

Despite significant advances in its economy and a burgeoning tourism industry 20% of Cambodians still live under the poverty line. Furthermore Cambodia has a reputation as one of the worst places in the world for child prostitution and human trafficking. The minimum monthly wage in Cambodia as well as Vietnam and Laos is currently under $150. By partnering with more social enterprises, which are empowering the locals in these countries through training and fair work opportunities, I am contributing to creating a sustainable future for them and their families.

Knowing that I can make a tangible difference to the lives of these trained artisans, by showcasing their creations, gives me that sense of fulfilment and satisfaction that I've been searching for since those university days. Their stories are now closely inter-weaved with my story. To be in a position whereby I can literally help them, their families and their wider communities out of poverty through my online store has brought me to a point in my life where I feel extremely fortunate to have found my life's purpose. This is success as I see it; this is the end goal, the sense of prosperity and personal growth, attained by doing well and giving back.

Temples and Markets presents a win-win for everybody involved – the artisans of course, the customers and for myself. It's simply a joyous feeling knowing you're contributing positively to the global community.

Life Feels Better For Me When I Help

Through a Women in Business networking group I have connected with several female entrepreneurs in recent times, who like myself have been fortunate to have found their life's purpose through their socially conscious businesses. Roz Campbell's story resonated with me greatly as her company Tsuno also helps disadvantaged women in developing countries.

How many of us have ever given a second thought to what women and girls do when they can't afford or don't have access to sanitary products? Roz had been researching the feminine hygiene market and heard about an Australian based charity providing education scholarships to girls in Sierra Leone, one of the world's poorest countries, called One Girl. After sending their first bunch of girls to school, they soon realised girls were missing up to a week of school every month because of their periods. They would fall behind at school, struggle in exams and eventually drop out.

Roz had heard heartbreaking stories of women resorting to rags, newspaper, kitchen sponges, leaves and sadly even tree bark as a feminine hygiene solution. Roz felt compelled to help because, in her own words,

> "Life Feels Better For Me When I Help,
>
> And This Is How I've Decided To Do So".

Roz sourced a sanitary product from a manufacturer working with sustainable fibres. They make bamboo and corn fibre disposable sanitary pads. The structure of the fibre is quite hollow, so it has lots of room for absorbing moisture, which is perfect for pads, drawing the moisture away from your body. In 2014 she ran a crowd funding campaign that saw 1400 women pre-ordering her sustainable and eco-friendly pads, giving her enough money for the first shipment. But Tsuno is much more than a company that sells fully sustainable disposable sanitary pads. Roz donates 50% of net profits from the sale of the Tsuno pads to charities helping to empower women in the developing world. She has an agreement with the One Girl charity that believes every girl on the planet has a right to education.

Roz's statement "Life feels better for me when I help" is such a simple phrase but it encompasses how I feel about success. By helping others we are helping ourselves.

Sally Maree Hetherington is a good friend of mine; we've become close through our aligned values. I connected with her after learning about her work for the Not for Profit organization Human and Hope Association based in Siem Reap, Cambodia. HHA empowers locals through training; education and community support so that they may create sustainable futures for themselves and break the cycle of poverty. Sally and I have partnered together to bring some of the handicrafts made by the Association's sewing graduates to my store.

Sally is a shining example of an inspiring successful woman in business. As she says, her success lies in the fact that she worked hard to actively put herself out of a job! From 2012 – 2016 Sally worked tirelessly as Operations Manager at Human and Hope Association, now entirely run by Cambodians. She always intended to step aside when the time was right leaving the locals to continue what she helped to build.

With the support of local staff Sally helped to build up the grassroots organization so that it was a professional, trustworthy and effective Non-Government Organisation for the community to reach out to donors for support. They registered Human and Hope Association as an official NGO, created a Khmer team of paid employees, developed a donor database, initiated various programs with the aim to alleviate social issues, initiated weekly training sessions, developed a sewing business and other sources of income and built a permanent location for HHA. Sally joined Human and Hope Association with the aim of helping the organization and staff reach their full potential, and then step back. She is incredibly proud of the achievements of her team and the fact that they have worked so hard that she could become redundant. She cried many tears the day she left, although she is still involved at board level for fundraising. But she insists selflessly it was never about her. It has always been about empowering the team with knowledge, skills and confidence so that she is no longer needed. If that's not the definition of success I don't know what is.

Life has, for me, gone full circle. I began my working life in department store retail buying and merchandising in the U.K. Fast forward 20 years later and I am living in Sydney but back in retail buying, this time sourcing for my own online store. But there's a stark contrast between then and now as today I am part of the growing movement of ethical retailers, and part of something good.

Successful Women In Business – Leadership Edition

The world is changing and consumers are becoming increasingly more conscious about their purchasing decisions, wanting to know where their purchases come from and who made them. Many larger fashion retailers are already recognizing this and endeavouring to treat their production workers ethically. Eventually the tide will flow against any who are still exploiting their workers.

It is clear that businesses with a purpose are the ones that achieve true success, not just success derived from an increasing profit margin. Whilst it is crucial to work towards a healthy profit margin if a business is to make a change in the world for good, that company must have a healthy perspective on what will benefit its customer, its suppliers and the community at large.

To have found my purpose at this stage in my life feels remarkable. The need to make a difference in the world had been staring me in the face from an early age and I've finally grabbed it. My personal success comes from the fulfilment I'm enjoying for the first time in my working life. There's immense satisfaction knowing I've made a woman feel good about herself when she wears a beautiful piece of unique jewellery I've sourced. In turn that same woman can enjoy the satisfaction of knowing she has contributed to the increased prosperity of the talented woman who made it.

In essence I am creating an ever-increasing circle of women who are affecting each other's lives in a positive way through trade. The more people whose lives I improve the more successful I will become. As long I am contributing to the increasing prosperity of the creative, strong and resilient artisans in the countries I love, the more fulfilled I will be.

"Success Isn't About How Much Money You Make. It's about the Difference you Make in People's Lives" a quote from Michelle Obama, USA First Lady 4/9/2012 DNC Convention.

By Judith Treanor

About The Author

Judith Treanor originates from a town close to London, England. Judith graduated in History at university before spending several years working in the Buying and Merchandising departments of House of Fraser, Harrods and Debenhams. Essentially she has been sourcing suppliers and product for over 25 years.

Successful Women In Business – Leadership Edition

In 1997 Judith left England as a slightly older than average backpacker to explore the world before migrating to Sydney, Australia. It was during those travels that the region of South East Asia found its special place in her heart and has never left.

Fast forward to the present and Judith is a proud mum to one amazing 12 year old son, who never fails to make her proud, and one floppy eared slightly crazy cocker spaniel cross. Judith practices Kundalini Yoga and is a serious foodie. She frequently gets itchy feet and travels overseas as often as she can. If she's near a beach Judith loves nothing more than taking a beach walk in the quiet of an early morning so she can make friends with the local dogs.

Travel, motherhood and serious illness have shaped who Judith is today. In 2006, aged 36 she was diagnosed with Breast Cancer, simultaneously the best and worst thing to have happened to her. Aware how short life is Judith is determined to live hers feeling healthy, contented and fulfilled. She has a fierce creative streak and an entrepreneurial nature.

She feels fortunate to have recently found her life's purpose - making a difference in the lives of others in the countries of S.E Asia that she fell in love with almost 20 years ago. She is now part of the growing ethical shopping movement. Judith's love of S.E Asia is showcased through her online store Temples and Markets which launched last November 2015.

You Can Contact Judith Via:

Email: contactus@templesandmarkets.com.au

Website: www.templesandmarkets.com

Social Media:

https://www.facebook.com/templesandmarkets

https://www.instagram.com/templesandmarkets

https://au.pinterest.com/templesmarkets/

Roz at Tsuno:

http://www.tsuno.com.au/

Sally at the Human and Hope Association:

http://www.sallyhetherington.com/

http://www.humanandhopeassociation.org/

Starting A Business With No Money

When I ask, "Why don't you start a business?" do you think to yourself, you need money to start a business and I don't have any? Most people do. There is a common misconception that you must have money to open a business and for lots of businesses you would be correct. You can't open a shop on the street corner without cash for deposits, bonds, fit outs, etc. But does that apply in all circumstances? No. Can you really start a business with very little or no money? Yes absolutely. Does it involve some creative problem and thinking outside the box? Yes. Are you capable of that? Absolutely!

My Story

I started my business with very, very little money to put down. Yes, there might have been a few rules I skirted around in order to get started, and I am not condoning rule and law breaking, but I have the philosophy of "Ready, Fire, Aim" approach to entrepreneurship rather than "Ready, Aim, Fire." I have always been the kind of person that gets very excited by new business ideas and becomes a bit like a bull at a gate. I just can't wait to get started on making money. I love seeing an idea come to reality and people actually start buying it. So exciting! Consequently I am a little bit lenient on details.

Some people have an approach to business that needs to lay out all the finer details before commencing on a project. Whilst I really admire those people and those skills are very necessary in certain fields, like engineering. I would like to think engineers plan minute details when they are building a bridge, things could really come undone for them if they just started and thought, "We will figure it out as we go."

We are lucky as entrepreneurs that we are allowed to be a little bit more flexible in our approach. So, we can have a brief plan and just get started, then we can adapt based on our customer's feedback and needs. Here is what I did: I used to make a lot of fresh juices at home. I loved doing my own juice cleanses at home. The fresh fruits and vegetables always made me feel amazing, snapping me out of bad eating habits, helping to remove bloating and made my skin glow. The benefits were always incredible, but the juicing and cleaning was always a hassle. I thought to myself, there has to be other people out there that would love the benefits of a juice cleanse without the hassle of making them.

So I decided to get started. First of all I had to design recipes and menus. Then I had to sort out packaging and design a "program" so there was a process for people to follow. I had to meet with naturopaths and nutritionists to help me design recipes and program types. I had to get samples of packaging that I could use. What did all this cost me? Time, but not money.

I used my home juicer and did the first juicing for a few weeks from my home very early in the morning, then did the deliveries before my day job. Then I would go into my recruitment job, and come home at night, answer any customer emails, etc. Then start again early the next morning. It was tiring, but I was so high on the adrenaline of actually making my own money in my own business that it didn't matter. I knew it wasn't going to be this way forever and growth was the first priority on my mind. It wasn't replacing my salary as I didn't pay myself a wage in the business until about 3 years in. But I wanted to grow and do it as organically as possible.

Just like that, I was in business! The free media trials have led to orders on my website and I had money in my PayPal account that I could use to buy packaging, and get proper labels printed and grow my business. It was such a fantastic feeling that I'd managed to start something that people were paying for, and it was such a rush to actually be in business!

How You Can Do It Too?

Start by finding your "genius". We all have value we can add to the world. Truly successful businesses are ones that genuinely add value to people's lives. Choose to approach your business as a method to share your genius with the world and add value to others, rather than looking at your business as a "get rich quick" scheme.

Questions To Ask Yourself?

What can I do really well? What can I do that would help other people enrich their lives? How can I do that with scale (help as many people as possible)? You don't have to only think in an altruistic sense, the value you could add could be done in a multitude of ways. Here are some examples to give you some perspective:

- A real estate investor provides affordable housing for people that can't afford to buy a property
- A hairdresser helps people look their best
- A learn to surf business helps people to find joy in doing something fun and exciting
- A nutrition consultant helps people feel their most energetic and vibrant
- An online fashion boutique owner helps people get the latest looks while shopping from the comfort of their home

Think about how you can add value to other people lives and where you can give your genius to the world.

The Key Is To Believe In What You Do...

Some people get freaked out by the idea of "selling". They will say to themselves, "oh, I could never do sales, I am not a salesperson." But the truth is we sell every day. The key is finding something you believe in so much that it doesn't even feel like selling. I recently met a lady who was so passionate for the product she sold that she just couldn't help herself trying to help people. She was a friend of a friend and we were away for the weekend.

Every single person we came across was an opportunity for her to help someone change their life. I was so impressed with her enthusiasm and thought if she talked to everyone she met in a day like that, when she bought petrol, groceries, went for a walk, picked the kids up from day care, and did this every day for 6 months, she would have touched so many potential customers for free. Her customers would then tell her friends and suddenly she has a market for her business with no advertising costs. The key is finding something that you really believe in. If you really believe you can truly add value to someone's life, and then you would not be "selling", you would be opening doors for people to change their lives.

When I was working full time, all I could think about was how insanely cool it would be and what an incredible rush it would be to have people actually spend their money on a product that I had created. I was working in a corporate job, wearing high heels and suits every day. I used to see myself in my comfy gym clothes as my job. I didn't want to be a personal trainer, but thought it would be so amazing if I had a job where I could wear what I wanted and be totally comfortable every day. This was a dream of mine, every day. Looking back I only really now realise the importance and gravity of my day dreaming. It was the consistent visualising and excitement that went with the imaginary pictures in my mind that manifested exactly what I dreamt about.

If business is what you want, then it is vital that you start living your life like it now. The importance of believing that you are already doing what you want, now. I don't mean going out and spending all your money in the belief that you already have loads of it. But, looking for opportunities, seeing things that you like other businesses doing and telling yourself that you will implement that in your business. Looking for marketing opportunities, looking at where your customers might congregate. You don't have to have an existing enterprise to do these things, you just need an idea and you can start acting as if you have the business already.

There is a book called, *The Magic of Believing*, by Claude M. Bristol. The ideas he presents are not new, it is in fact quite an old book, but I love the way he presents his perspective on how things have happened for him based on setting his new beliefs about his life, career, etc.

So visualise your new life running a successful business, what kind of person would you be? How would you hold yourself? How would you explain your business when you meet new people? How would you dress? What kind of books would you read? What kind of websites/networking groups would you be part of? How would your new life make you feel? Creating a new reality for yourself is a crucial step to becoming the business owner you want to be.

Marketing Your Business

The basis of any successful business is marketing. A lot of people will argue the basis is sales, or customers, but you won't have any of those if your customers don't know about you. The only way they will know about you is marketing. Now the idea of a marketing plan probably freaks a lot of people out, and rightly so. When I was doing my MBA and had to prepare marketing plans, they were a lot of work, a very detailed, very densely worded, a thickly bound document that looked great on a shelf but was never looked at again. You will need to have a very basic and simple understanding of marketing for your business. But it can be very simple, so don't panic. Here are the most important questions to address:

What Makes Me Different?

This is called defining your Unique Selling Proposition (USP). It is why you are special compared to other peoples, what makes your product better than others, why should people spend their hard earned money on your product as opposed to someone else's. For my business, in the early stages I was the only juice cleanse company. So while it may seem that my USP was easy, it wasn't. A lot of people thought it was kind of crazy spending $300 on 5 day's worth of juice.

But my USP was focused on providing a very easy and very healthy way for people to cleanse their body, feel amazing and kick-start to a healthier lifestyle. Don't be afraid that your USP will change as your business evolves. A natural part of the business life cycle is competition, so as your business grows so will your competition. That may be direct replicas of your product or it may be competition for the consumer spend, for example as my business grew, direct competitors popped up with the same ideas offering the same products as my company did. As well as other options for people to do a detox program with things like herbs, AND options for people to do their own juicing at home. So I had to start providing something unique for my customers that was different to my direct and indirect competition. Now that business has changed our USP focuses on providing the freshest juice as we are still the only business offering daily delivery within 20km of CBD in Sydney, Melbourne and Brisbane.

Who Are My Customers?

You need to understand exactly the type of person that will buy from you. Are they just like you? Or completely different from you? What are their main motivations to buy? Is it because they want the latest fashions or perhaps they are a practical dresser that prefers to spend their money on computer games. Are they male or female? What kind of job do they have? What would they do on a Saturday night? Would they be out at the trendiest night spots or at home in bed after an exhausting day with the kids? Put yourself in your customer's shoes and really understand who they are. This is a really key step on your marketing plan. Once you have understood your customer you can better know where they will be and what they will do. So not only can you tailor your product/offering accordingly, you can spend your marketing dollars more efficiently and effectively as opposed to spending a lot of money in a blanket approach.

What Do I Need To Say To Those Customers To Help Win Business Or Maintain Business?

Ok, now you have figured WHO your customers are, you understand how they tick, what they like and dislike, you can now figure out the message that you want to send to them. Don't be afraid to have different messages for different customers. For some people you might want to say something particular, and for another group of people it might be a different message.

How Am I Going To Get In Contact With Those Customers?

This is all about the how you are going to get your message across to your customers. So, it could be via social media, or TV advertising (if you have the budget!), maybe leaflet drops if you are a pizza place in a particular suburb, it could be calling childcare centres to get your sample products in the hands of time poor mums if you have a product that might help them. Be prepared to think laterally when you don't have a big budget. Once you completed the step of identifying your customer there might be something that your customer does that you can piggy back off, like do they do Yoga each week, so call the yoga studios and do a deal with them.

Building Credibility

It's important to build credibility in your area of expertise, whether it is selling beauty products online or if you are a consultant for helping women achieve financial freedom. The easiest and cheapest way I have found to do this is blogging. Remember you don't have to position yourself as an "expert" on a particular topic, so don't stress that you don't have a degree or any qualifications, but you can definitely join the conversation. Use your blog to discuss current happenings in your arena, new research, what you do (e.g. your daily skincare routine, or your home recipes), your own experience with experts, etc. I don't have qualifications in nutrition or naturopathic remedies, although I consulted with them and used them heavily I was very self-educated on the topics. I read, read and re-read all the latest and greatest books on topics of natural health. So although I wasn't an "expert" I still felt that I was able to join the conversation and discuss theories, add in my opinion and my own experience.

Blogging only takes your time and your thinking. You can easily and quickly add additional credibility to your website or profile or store via blogging. You can add to your search rankings too with more material on your topic, so the search engines will love you.

My Tips For Starting A Business As Cost Effectively As Possible

Define your marketing plan as above – it may take some time to think about, but it will be the best and most profitable exercise you can do.

Starting The Website – look at the free builder options available. Just search "free website builder" in your search engine and you will find there are quite a few basic options out there to get started. These days they are very easy to find your way through and to start developing. Remember you don't have to start with all the bells and whistles, just get started you can always upgrade later when you have some money in the bank.

Using PayPal – setting up a payment gateway can be expensive and fiddly, but the easiest and quickest way to start accepting money on your site is PayPal. It is a recognised brand and people feel comfortable with it, the merchant fees aren't the best, but once again, it is a great option to just get cracking and then you can spend some time setting up a different merchant gateway when you are more established.

Free Media Coverage – it's as simple as making a call. This was definitely a clincher for me in the early days, getting my product in the hands of media influencers I did by contacting PR agencies and media, it's just call away. I called all the magazines and asked for the beauty editor, I explained I had a juice cleanse that I really wanted them to try so it would be amazing if I could send them a free trial.

Be honest, act with integrity, share love and you will be rewarded. They are just people and they are always looking for new material to write about in magazines, so sell your products with your passion and they will be excited to write about it.

Asking Suppliers Questions – if you need samples, testers, etc.. Don't be afraid to ask your potential suppliers for samples. They are in business too, so you as a potential new customer could be great news for them. They may not be willing, but you will be surprised at how many could be. You just need to ask.

Use Social Media – Using Twitter and Instagram are great ways to promote your product free of charge using hashtags. Set up your accounts for free and educate yourself a little on how the whole hashtag game works and you can start getting followers and people liking your posts. It all helps to spread the word.

Conclusion

Starting a business without much money is an achievable and rewarding path to success. Anyone that believes in themselves, and believes in their goals, like I did, can find their way into their own exciting venture. Find your own genius and create value for other people and you will find yourself skyrocketing to success.

By Catherine Craig

About The Author

Catherine Craig is the owner of Schkinny Maninny. She has been in business almost a decade and started her company from scratch to million dollar plus revenues without any debt. She believes in healthy eating and clean lifestyle and how juicing can change your life.

If You Would Like Some More Info Please Just Send Me A Message:

Email: catherine@schkinnymaninny.com.au

Finding Out What Being Successful Really Means

Running my own business was not my plan. Running my own mediation and conflict management business was certainly never my plan. When I graduated with my law degree, I thought I would be an employee solicitor for most of my working life. My aspirations were modest: I wanted a job I enjoyed and that I was good at, to help people through difficult times in their lives; to appear in court, present cases and get results for my clients; and to live a rich and fulfilling life outside of work. In 2012 I achieved all of that, but it was not making me feel happy or "successful". I felt at times that my life was passing me by while I did what was expected of me. I had worked hard to get where I was, but it wasn't right for me.

Outwardly I was on the "path to success", if success meant a secure job, higher than average salary and prospects to progress up the ranks of a law firm. I thought my success was bound up in my work, my status as a lawyer, and my financial standing. Since leaving that life and pursuing my own business I have learned that success has nothing to do with the job you hold, how much you earn, where you live or how often you eat out. Success is about who you are as a person and how you act towards others and towards yourself.

Becoming a lawyer had not been an easy path for me. In high school I decided that I wanted to study law at university and set my focus on getting into a "good" university. Years later I found some of my primary school mementos, which showed that even at the age of 5 when asked what I wanted to be when I grew up I had answered "a lawyer". I suspect it was because of the nice lawyer on *A Country Practice*. Like most kids I cycled through all sorts of other career choices including mounted police officer and mechanic (like Charlene in *Neighbours* – do you sense a theme here?). But by middle high school I had cycled back to becoming a lawyer.

When the university entrance scores were released I was aiming for 85+ to get in to law at my choice of university. I didn't think I would get the 90+ required for the top tier universities, but I was confident of getting in to one of my top two preferences. I opened my envelope and the bottom fell out of my world. 77. I had got a score of 77, nowhere near the score I needed; I felt like a complete failure and was inconsolable that first day. Soon after the score came out, the first round of university placement offers were made. All my preferences had been to study law combined with either arts or performing arts (my grand plan had been to study acting to enhance my court room skills), and to my surprise I was offered a spot; but it was for a university in Armidale, NSW. I didn't know anyone in Armidale; it was hours and hours away from home, and it snowed in the winter.

I did not want to spend the next 5 years of my life in Armidale. My preferred options were Canberra and Wollongong. Both cities were closer to my home town, and I had family in Wollongong, plus it is close to Sydney and is on the beach. I researched my options and I took a risk: I applied to study arts at the University of Wollongong, with a plan to earn high enough marks in my first year to transfer into law in the second year. My gamble paid off, and in hindsight, it was the best decision I could have made.

My birthday is 31st March, and I started school aged 4-turning-5, which meant that when I arrived for Orientation Week at UoW I was still 17 years old. This was going to be a year of fun and success. I enrolled in all the subjects I just knew I was going to love and excel in: French, Acting, Psychology, Music and a few law subjects on offer for the Commerce students, to get a head start on my plan to switch to law. By the end of the year I had learned so much, including that I was not enjoying studying French at tertiary levels and was not very good at it; I was not cut out for the 3 year Creative Arts (Acting) degree; and I love psychology.

My plan had been to transfer into an Arts/Law degree, majoring in psychology, but that required me to take other humanities subjects as well as psychology, and I hadn't found anything else I wanted to pursue at that level. Towards the end of my first year the university announced a new degree: Bachelor of Science majoring in Psychology. This degree was structured to allow students to focus purely on psychology subjects or combine them with other scientific disciplines. This was exactly what I wanted to do, study law and psychology and drop my other humanities subjects. I applied and was accepted. I was granted advanced standing for the psych and law subjects I had taken in first year, and was able to progress with my peers in the psychology stream. This was an option that had not existed when I was making my selections at the end of high school. Had I not taken the risk to start an arts degree and move into law from there, but instead accepted the offer to study arts/law at Armidale, who knows how things would have turned out.

Studying law was a mixed bag. Some subjects I enjoyed others I detested; I excelled in some, others were a real struggle. One summer a friend and I enrolled in Summer School with Southern Cross University. I don't remember how we found out about it, but the big appeal was that the 1 week intensive courses were held in Byron Bay. My mum, sister and some of our extended family were living in Ballina, about 30 minutes' drive from Byron, so I packed up my 1977 red Mini and, with my sister as co-driver, we road tripped from Wollongong to Ballina over 2 days.

My friend Rachel flew up and we had a great week in Byron studying the laws of war with a leading scholar in the field, who went on to become Director for International Law and Policy at the International Committee of the Red Cross (ICRC) in Geneva. I stayed on for an extra week for an intensive on psychology, psychiatry and the law, with a leading Melbourne barrister who has since been appointed as Queens Counsel, a Professorial Fellow in Law and Psychiatry at the University of Melbourne, and an Adjunct Professor of Law and Forensic Medicine at Monash University. At the time it was a chance to mix a beach side holiday with knocking over 2 subjects towards my law degree. The essay I wrote for the international laws of war subject became the foundation for my Honours Thesis: *From Charlemagne to Geneva – the*

History of the Laws of War. I graduated from my Bachelor of Laws (Honours)/Bachelor of Science (Psychology) in 2001 right around the time I landed my first full time job as a law clerk with a small firm in Helensburgh. For 12 months I drove the 30 minute commute each way to my job, and then spent evenings and weekends attending classes and completing assignments for my Graduate Diploma of Legal Practice (NSW having done away with articled clerks years earlier). I was finally admitted to practice in February 2003, 7 years after enrolling at UoW. In November that year I married Sam, who had supported me through my honours and graduate diploma, and remains my partner in all things.

Over the next 5 years I worked in 2 firms, learning a lot along the way both about the practice of law and the management of staff. In 2007 I was an Associate of my firm with an interesting and challenging portfolio of work. I was making budget and informally mentoring staff. I was being given the opportunity to take on more and more responsibility and to build a name for myself; but I wasn't happy and neither were others in the office. There has been instability in the firm with high turnover and a partner resigning to begin his own speciality practice. Tensions were high, morale was low, and junior staff came to me for mentoring, support and to voice their concerns. As a lawyer I was able to talk to the partners informally and let them know about the mood of the office.

On a personal level, I didn't see myself as a litigation lawyer forever, and had been considering other options. I was interested in learning more about frontline management (Sam had done a frontline management diploma as part of his job and it seemed a valuable set of tools for lawyer-managers, and something that was sorely missing from the industry), but with the previous redundancies still fresh in my mind, I began to think about other ways I could be a "fee earner" for my firm as well as a manager and struck upon the idea of being accredited as a mediator so I could be charged out by the firm, but not so weighed down in case work that I wouldn't be able to support and assist staff. And then I was promoted to Associate of the firm and the idea remained that, just an idea.

Successful Women In Business – Leadership Edition

Roll around to 2012 and I was in another role that ticked all the boxes on my wish list, at least on paper. I was fit and slim, and I went to the gym regularly. I was in the best physical shape I had been since high school. I was living in Melbourne, the most liveable city in the world. I had a circle of friends who were also professionals making their way in the world. But I was once again – or perhaps still – feeling unsatisfied, unhappy and unsuccessful.

I was working as an in-house lawyer for a company that was undergoing a restructure and "culture change program". Morale was low as all around us colleagues' positions were being made redundant. At one stage our floor was only half occupied and later an entire floor was closed to save on overheads. A colleague and I used to commiserate "love the work, hate the workplace", but this had been the case for my last 3 jobs. Maybe the issue was me?

In May 2012 my uncle Bob died after years slowly dying as cancer ravaged his body. We had celebrated his birthday 6 months earlier with a huge family gathering, a bittersweet party that we all knew would be his last. My extended family is not large, and of all my aunts and uncles, I had been closest to him and his family. They were the ones living in Wollongong when I moved there for Uni, and they looked after me when I was a country kid lost in the bustling city (literally and figuratively).

I spend a summer living with them when I didn't want to leave my Wollongong friends and go back to a hometown that held little for me anymore. For a time Sam and I had lived around the corner from them, and we were regularly shared Sunday dinners and family gatherings. He was only 65 years old when he died; I was 34. I returned from his funeral in Wollongong and went back to work. The first conversation with my boss went along the lines of "I know you've been out of the office and have emails and things to catch up on, so instead of our usual 10am file review meeting, let's move it to 2pm so you have time to get caught up." No sympathy, no questions about how the funeral had been or the trip to Wollongong and back, not even how was I feeling, just business as usual. That was the first clue that the issue was not *entirely* me.

As the "culture change program" rolled on and more redundancies were announced, it became clear that the company's values no longer aligned with my own. We were being asked to do more with less, and when we raised concerns over ethical and professional standards, the non-lawyers on the executive dismissed our concerns. Lawyers in other departments were being made redundant and their roles given to non-lawyers who did not have the technical knowledge and skills required to do the job. There was a very real fear that our entire department would be cut and our work outsourced to private firms.

I didn't want to stay in that job but I didn't want to start over again at another firm in another job. I felt like a failure and a fraud. I felt I had tried everything – working for privates firms, federal and state government, and in-house as a corporate lawyer - and that being a lawyer was just not for me. I had worked hard to get where I was and it was gut wrenching to think that I may have been on the 'wrong path' all along. I now know that there is no such thing as "the wrong path", but at the time it was daunting and I felt I had wasted a good portion of my life pursuing the wrong dream.

I started to think about other options. What else could I do? What else did I want to do? The idea of qualifying as a mediator bubbled back to the surface of my mind. I was working in-house in a role that would not allow me to be hired out as a mediator with fees paid to the company, so I asked to reduce my position from full time to part time, giving me a day or two to pursue outside interests. Obviously I expected to have my salary reduced pro rata. I pointed to working mums who had returned to the office part time after their maternity leave, and assured my manager that I would be available for court dates, mediations and other commitments that could not be rescheduled. My request was denied. I was told the company could not afford for me to be part time in addition to the working mums.

It all became too much for me. I felt unappreciated, unsupported and undervalued. In the course of a teary meeting with my manager she asked "are you resigning?" I looked at her and said "I think I am." I was coming up to my 35th birthday. My Uncle Bob had died at the age of 65. If I only had 30 years left on this planet, I was not going to spend them being miserable in a job that was not satisfying me, even though I had invested the last 17 years in to that career path.

In February 2013, 10 years and a day after my admission to practice, I said goodbye to my colleagues and walked away from my job as a lawyer. I wondered if I was walking away from the law altogether. One of my mottos in life is "never say never"; but on that day I was confident my mediation business would take off quickly and that I would soon be too busy and too wildly successful to think about returning to the practice of law.

Later that month I began my mediation accreditation course at Monash Uni and passed my exams a few months later. Mid 2013 I launched my business, with a website I had designed myself and business cards and stationary by a graphic designer. In September 2013 I received my National Mediator Accreditation. I was ready.

I now refer to 2013 as my "Gap Year". As well as studying for my mediation qualifications, I redoubled my efforts and completed the Diploma in Fashion Styling I had begun while still in my corporate job. I had signed up for a 6 month online self-paced course; 2 years later I held that diploma in my hand, and I am just as proud of it as I am of my Law and Science degrees. It represents a lot of time and effort, not only to complete the course work and assessments, but also a lot of work on myself. Since then I have learned the value of more formal and structured 'self-development' but at that time, I enjoyed the chance to reflect on what made me happy and what didn't; what I wanted from my work life and what I did not.

A friend was teaching at a local university, and needed tutors; so I taught sociology of health to first year nursing students for a year. I landed a job as store manager for a Sydney fashion designer opening her first Melbourne store (that job came to a shuddering halt when I suggested that she really ought to pay staff at award wages and pointed out her obligations under Fair Work; the next week I was restructured out of the job). And I tinkered away at the mediation business, certain that it was about to take off.

Learning About Business

I sent out letters and emails letting people know I was now open for business and waited for the bookings to come pouring in; and waited; and waited. It turns out that "If you build it they will come" is not a sound business plan.

I did webinars and online courses, read articles and joined Facebook groups. I went along to networking events and when the Small Business Festival rolled around in August, I attended several seminars and workshops. I was still teaching, and eventually took on some casual customer service work to help pay the bills.

Even though I was doing everything as cheaply as possible – I won my first headshots package in a competition on Facebook - the business was costing me time, money and effort for little reward. I cringed inwardly every time someone asked me how the business was going. "Slowly but surely" I answered cheerily, but the truth was, it was not going. I had a few paying customers from time to time, but I was not attracting the right – or enough – people. I was still not "successful".

I now think of 2014 as a year of learning – learning about websites, search engine optimisation, marketing, advertising, book keeping, accounting, networking, referral relationships and sundry other things necessary when running your own business. Early in my legal career I had decided not to pursue my dream of becoming a barrister when I realised they essentially ran their own small business from top to bottom and, unlike on the British TV shows I had grown up watching, their clerks did not find them clients or handle their office administration. Ironically, here I was, 10 years later, learning all the things that had turned me off about life at the bar.

My First Mentor

Somewhere along the line I was feeling frustrated and sorry for myself, and complained to a brilliant networker I know that I was just not meeting the right people – being the kind of people who wanted to hire me. She suggested I join a particular Facebook Group, which I did. The group is run by a business mentor, speaker and author who provides support to women like me, wanting to build the business and life of their dreams but who are a bit stuck. I followed along the posts in the group and I took up some of the challenges and absorbed some of the lessons.

I went along to some workshops she ran in Melbourne, and then I joined an exclusive Mastermind group with 2 other business owners. For 6 months we met weekly, learning, growing and stretching ourselves. Out Mentor pushed us and challenged us. She helped me to uncover some underlying beliefs that were holding me back in business, and encouraged me to be more myself when promoting and acting in my business. Slowly I peeled away the lawyer layers.

Instead of the stiff photos in my suits I started appearing in more relaxed clothing that reflect my personality and style. I realised that one of my key strengths is my ability to explain complex and daunting legal concepts and procedure in plain English. It took about 4 months, but she eventually broke me of the "Hourly rate, pay after the work is done" mind-set (classic 6-minute-unit lawyer thinking) and helped me understand and embrace ways to package up my services and to get paid up front.

She got me to think about new and innovative ways of delivering my services so that, instead of sharing my knowledge and expertise 1-to-1 I could share it with many at the same time. She helped me turn my business around, from the inside out.

My Path Is My Own

Of course, I now know I wasn't "on the wrong path", but rather, that some paths are more circuitous than others. The truth is, without my years studying and practicing law, I may never have fallen in love with mediation or ever branched out on my own. During my lawyering years I often threatened to "quit my job and sell dresses in a shop somewhere". Well I did that, and it wasn't any better.

What is "success" anyway? When I graduated from university I thought "success" was position, reputation and salary. When I launched my business, I defined "success" as a certain number of clients bringing a defined amount of money.

My goal was and remains to support Sam and myself so that he has the freedom to focus on his academic research and to work as, when and how he wants, not take jobs for purely financial reasons. It didn't happen straight away, and it hasn't happened yet, but I remain confident that it will happen, we will get there. But my financial goals are not the only measure of my success.

Now I define "success" differently. Success for me is a general level of happiness and contentment in my daily life. Success is sleeping well at night, knowing that tomorrow is a new day filled with new possibilities. Success is celebrating the small wins – a leader in my industry "liked" a photo or post I shared on Facebook; I helped someone get through a really difficult situation; I received a lovely testimonial or thank you email.

Success is being able to go to a movie at 10am on a Monday with my husband and an out of town friend, just because we can. Success is being able to set aside the day to day busyness of my business and to be there when my friends needs me – which I have been able to do twice this year, and will continue to do.

When the opportunity came up to write for this book on Successful Woman in Business a whisper of doubt said "you can't write a chapter on being successful in business because your business is still so new and not yet self-sufficient"; but that was not the point of this book. This book is about celebrating successful women, women who happen to be in business for themselves, and by any measure I am a successful woman.

My amazing husband and I have been married for over 12 years. Together we have moved house, jobs and states; we have travelled far and wide as well as explored our own backyard; we have faced triumph and tragedy together and I know that we have many more adventures ahead of us. We have some truly wonderful friends who are a constant source of strength and support, as are our families.

We live in inner city Melbourne with our pet rabbit who brings us joy and laughter every day. I have a balcony garden in which I grow food for us and our rabbit, and worm farms to help recycle some of our vegetable scraps and reduce our contribution to landfill. I make my own clothes, and mend, alter or recycle other garments into something new, further reducing my carbon footprint.

Friends trust me to care for their children, and permit me the honour of having some small hand in their growth and development. In return, I share my loves with those children: comic books, music, rabbits, fashion; and I share my values with them: feminism, equity, democracy, and self-determination, truth, honesty and integrity.

Running my own business was never my plan in life, but neither was being in a job without joy or satisfaction. My goal in life if to "be happy" and every day I take conscious steps to make that my reality. I may not be making a fortune in my business – yet – but I have contentment, satisfaction, ethical standards and values; I love and am loved; I have a positive impact in others' lives; and in all of that I am successful.

By Rebecca Carroll-Bell

About The Author

Rebecca Carroll-Bell – The Everyday Mediator

Mediator, lawyer and conflict management specialist Rebecca Carroll-Bell helps people from all walks of life to eliminate drama and overcome conflict in their everyday lives. Using everyday language and techniques learned through her observation and study of human behaviour in and out of the court room, Rebecca brings a fresh approach to issues as diverse as family and divorce, workplace conflict and neighbourhood disputes.

Successful Women In Business – Leadership Edition

A successful litigation lawyer for over 10 years, Rebecca brings her extensive negotiation skills and experience to conflict management and resolution situations. Described as "a great all-rounder – an attentive listener and a witty contributor" Rebecca's background in psychology and law allow her to nurture her clients when they need a little bit of emotional topping up, while keeping them accountable and calling them out on their junk.

For further information please contact: 0411770125

Rebecca@rcbmediationservices.com.au

Rebecca Carroll-Bell is The Everyday Mediator – passionate about managing, resolving and preventing conflict in everyday life: everydaymediator

Find Rebecca Online At:

Website http://www.rcbmediationservices.com.au

LinkedIn https://au.linkedin.com/pub/rebecca-carroll-bell/25/580/1a

Facebook https://www.facebook.com/RCBMediationServices

Twitter https://twitter.com/RCBMediation

Google+ https://www.google.com/+RCBMediatorWestMelbourne

Instagram https://www.instagram.com/bec_cb/

Successful Women In Business – Leadership Edition

THE ENERGY HEALING MAGAZINE

The Energy Healing Magazine

The Energy Healing Magazine is an independent online publication which prides itself in being the first-choice resource for readers seeking a greater understanding of energy healing and also to participate more actively in natural health and wellness.

We work tirelessly to always inspire, educate, and empower our readers, partners, and professional colleagues either via our podcasts, articles, awards and product reviews.

The Energy Healing Magazine is not a news magazine. Rather, we are an online magazine produced with **CARE** (Commentary, Analysis, Reflection and Experience). Our readers value our content because it provides them with insight from some of the most knowledgeable energy healing practitioners in the world.

Our mission is to provide insights and information about all forms of energy healing & natural products in order to improve the quality of life physically, mentally, emotionally and spiritually.

Updated 24 hours a day, 7 days a week, we deliver relevant, incisive, high-quality content that not only offers advice and insight but also informed analyses of issues relevant to people living and working not only in the UK but around the world.

www.theenergyhealingmagazine.com

Successful Women In Business – Leadership Edition

Successful Women In Business – Leadership Edition

Printed in Poland
by Amazon Fulfillment
Poland Sp. z o.o., Wrocław